THE FUND THEORY OF ACCOUNTING AND ITS IMPLICATIONS FOR FINANCIAL REPORTS

By
WILLIAM J. VATTER

THE UNIVERSITY OF CHICAGO PRESS
CHICAGO AND LONDON

Standard Book Number: 226-85151-6

THE UNIVERSITY OF CHICAGO PRESS, CHICAGO 60637
The University of Chicago Press, Ltd., London

Published 1947. Sixth Impression 1969
Printed in the United States of America

PREFACE

This little excursion into some untried and rather speculative areas of accounting thought is the formulation of a set of hypotheses which may deserve further development, perhaps some amount of actual application, in the field of accounting practice. It is an attempt to set up a framework around which the ideas of accounting may have better and fuller expression and from which may develop a broader application of certain accounting techniques which now have but limited uses.

The notions that are presented in the following pages arise from many sources, and many persons have contributed in one way or another to the work which has been done; this discussion is the product of many hands and minds, although it is reported from but a single point of view. To give credit to all those who deserve mention would involve listing a great many names—teachers and colleagues, assistants and associates, even friends and acquaintances—who have each played some part in making this discussion what it is. The very length of such a list, however, would defeat its purpose.

My greatest debt is owed to those who have reasoned against my own views; whatever merit may appear in this presentation is the direct result of the stimulation thus provided; the shortcomings of this work arise from my own unwillingness to follow their good advice.

William J. Vatter

TABLE OF CONTENTS

CHAPTER I

ORIGINS OF THE FUND THEORY

Every science, methodology, or other body of knowledge is oriented to some conceptual structure—a pattern of ideas brought together to form a consistent whole or a frame of reference to which is related the operational content of that field. Without some such integrating structure, procedures are but senseless rituals without reason or substance; progress is but a fortunate combination of circumstances; research is but fumbling in the dark; and the dissemination of knowledge is a cumbersome process, if indeed there is any "knowledge" to convey.

In the physical sciences hypotheses have been formulated, tested, and applied in rigorous sequence; the underlying structure of ideas remains ever present, even as it evolves from one stage to another through continuing experiment. However, it should be emphasized that, although the structure of ideas in these fields is affected by the statistical evidence arising from experiment, the experiments do not in themselves establish theory. Rather, they provide tests for hypotheses. Sometimes, of course, the results of experiments suggest new arrangements of ideas to explain the findings, and amendments of previous theories may ensue. The structures of knowledge are not immutable, and no theory is ever to be accepted or rejected without reservation. Basic hypotheses evolve continually into new, more complete, and more satisfactory forms; at a given time there may be a number of alternative theories with respect to new data. The continuous formulation, testing, and evaluation of hypotheses is but a stage in the integration of theory, and the process of assimilating new ideas into the structures of theory is the growth and fruition of knowledge.

Accounting—despite its origin and development in the "practical" world of business—is a methodology based upon a similar structure of ideas, however crude or imperfectly understood. The development of accounting thought follows a pattern basically no different from that of the physical sciences. There are systems of thought which underlie accounting processes to provide rational bases for the activities in which accountants engage. However far these systems of ideas may seem to fall short of scientific standards, they do underlie the practices of accounting; and the testing, reformulation, and dissemination of these patterns of thinking are the means by which accounting achieves progress.

There are some who argue that accounting is not, and cannot be logical; they point out that "the rules of accounting, even more than those of the law, are the product of experience rather than of logic."[1] This view cannot be accepted here. Although it is true that experience is the only real basis for generalization in any field of knowledge, it is also true that experience is itself an interpretation; and this involves the analysis and appraisal of data or conduct in terms of some kind of standard. The threads of logical thought are an essential part of practice; they serve to bind observations together into those simple generalizations which we call "facts."[2] The theoretical basis for accounting must be a logical one, even though experience may be the only final test of its validity. And, however much it may be colored by convention, evolved through trial and error in practice, or even tainted with expediency in application, the logical structure of theory that underlies accounting serves to orient the field and to systematize those processes and procedures related to financial reports.

Starting from this premise, the purpose of the present discussion is to outline one approach to such a basic structure of ideas—the fund theory—in contradistinction to other frames of reference which have been proposed. It is not intended that this presentation will be exhaustive; indeed, certain questions will be considered only to the extent that they relate directly to the basic structure which is being proposed. For instance, terminology is so important an element of any theoretical structure that some aspects of it must be discussed; yet it is undesirable, perhaps even useless, to attempt stringent definitions here for more than a few fundamental concepts. Despite the importance of valuation in any discussion of financial accounting, this subject will be referred to in these pages only to the extent that is essential to establish or clarify certain issues. The routines associated with given account classifications (and the problems of analysis and allocation which they entail) cannot be dealt with exhaustively in a study of the present scope; but some aspects of this necessarily must be considered to make clear the picture that is to be presented. The discussion is to a large extent exploratory and general in nature; it cannot be aimed at the solution of all problems of accounting, although it might serve to point the way toward a better solution of some of them. The most that can be accomplished here is to present a basis for a theoretical structure; its complete application and development must remain for some future effort.

At this writing there are two different schools of thought which are made to serve as integrating framework for accounting theory. Each of these has gained some recognition, and both are actually applied in accounting practice. The older of these—known as the "proprietary" or the "representative" theory—dates from at least the beginning of the nineteenth century; it is the first structure that is now recognized as such, if indeed it is not the original basis for accounting methodology.[3] The second viewpoint—called the "entity" school—is of comparatively recent origin.[4] To establish a basis for the presentation to be attempted here, it is advisable to review some of the salient features of these two schools of thought.[5]

The essence of the proprietary theory may be expressed in the following terms: accounting records and statements are maintained and prepared from the standpoint of the proprietor of a business enterprise, and they are aimed at a measurement of and the analysis of changes in the proprietor's "net worth." In this scheme the assets are the proprietor's property; liabilities are the proprietor's debts; and the emphasis of accounting is focused upon profit—in the sense of accretions to the proprietorship that arise from the operations of the enterprise. This system of ideas did fit the facts of the case fairly well when businesses and other enterprises were organized as individual "proprietorships"; and the notion of profit thus involved was a useful and workable one. The operations of the business unit commenced with the investment of the proprietor, and his connection with the business was continuous, from the inception of operations until the venture was brought to a close. Originally, there was good sense in the position that accounting operated for the benefit and for the information of the proprietor, because this was then in fact the almost universal pattern of business organization. Even in the case of general or limited partnerships, the interest of the proprietors was generally coextensive with their investment in, and their withdrawal from, the firm. The legal rule, that a change in the personnel of the partnership terminated one venture and started another, helped further to maintain the distinct relations between "owner-investment" and the operations of accounting.

It is to be noted that in the proprietary theory, as well as in the entity theory, the business firm is the center or the area of attention. No extended argument is necessary to establish that the area of attention for a given set of records and reports must be limited. The operations and the organization of financial and economic activity are far too complex to have much meaning unless they are viewed in terms of a specified unit of activity, some particular set of interests, or some specific problem. The fact that the organization of society actually is expressed and achieved in terms of enterprise units affords a basis for this kind of restriction or delimitation. Hence, both proprietary theory and entity theory recognize the independence of certain activities from each other for accounting purposes; and the unit of accounting under either theory is the business venture or enterprise. However, to define the area of attention in terms of an enterprise merely restricts the *scope* of a set of books or a series of reports; the way in which materials are dealt with within them is quite another matter. For the proprietary theorist the proprietor is the person to whom and for whom reports are made, and the concepts of net worth and profit are personal ideas, in that the proprietor's interest is the axis around which the processes of accounting revolve. This view is expressed in varying degrees of emphasis by various writers; perhaps the best illustration of the way in which the proprietary view gains expression is the following statement of Sprague's:

> Thus the right hand side of the balance sheet is entirely composed of claims against or rights over the left side. "Is it not then true," it may be asked, "that the right hand side is entirely composed of liabilities?" The answer to this is that the rights of others, or the liabilities, differ materially from the rights of the proprietor.[6]

The advent of the corporate form of business enterprise marks a change in the basic pattern, because corporate proprietorship is quite a different kind of thing from the simpler forms of business units. Except for the "closed" corporation (which is really nothing more than a partnership clothed with the legal attributes of corporate form), the proprietary interest is not that of one or a few men, but it refers to a constantly changing group of people. Stockholders typically do not "invest" directly in the corporate enterprise; rather, they acquire shares by transfer from predecessors, by means of exchange transactions that appear in the financial records of the enterprise only in terms of share entries made in the stockholders' ledgers. The continuity of interest characteristic of the simpler forms of organization is broken in the corporate form, and the notion of ownership becomes a complex and shifting concept.

The idea of profit that fits the case of sole proprietorship and partnership begins to break down when it is applied to proprietors who come and go as shares are exchanged. The determination of profit under proprietary theory involves the measurement of proprietary net worth at two points in time; that is, the change in investment of the proprietor over time is established by the measurement of net worth at the beginning and the close of the period. The fact that interim bookkeeping segregates the current transactions from the proprietary equity at the beginning of the period merely emphasizes this point. But the corporate proprietorship (so far as the stockholders are concerned) arises from numerous investments made at various times; measuring profit for individual stockholders becomes an impossibly tedious problem. But there is more difficulty than this. The real trouble arises from the fact that the "investments" of corporate stockholders take place in a market in which the prices of shares reflect anticipations as to the future of corporate activity. Such prices cannot be the same as the book value of the investments, unless those market anticipations are completely and directly reflected in the accounts of the corporation. This would mean constant revision of valuations as the market prices of shares changed, as well as the recognition of valuation factors which are not always too clear even in the minds of those who buy or sell the shares. Again, it must be recognized that the normal situation in such markets is one of continuously changing prices; these reflect individual as well as collective differences in the anticipations of buyers and sellers. The result is that the accountant who attempts to apply proprietary theory to the corporate situation is placed in an impossible situation. He must either reflect and record all the changes that occur in the market anticipations reflected in the prices of shares (adjusting and revising the valuation of proprietorship as a whole), or his record of "investment" will have little or no meaning to the individual stockholders. The simple notion of profit expressed as the personal gain of the proprietor cannot be applied to the corporate situation in which owner-stockholders are constantly moving in and out of the area of proprietary interest.

This state of affairs lays the scene for the entity theory of accounting. Entity theory does not differ with proprietary theory as to the area to which attention is to be devoted in carrying on the accounting for business enterprise; but it does involve a decidedly different viewpoint as to what kinds of things shall be given emphasis, and what point of view is to be maintained, in carrying on accounting operations or in preparing financial reports. The basic position of the entity theorist is perhaps best expressed in the following terms:

> The business undertaking is generally conceived of as an entity or institution in its own right, separate and distinct from the parties who furnish the funds, and it has become almost axiomatic that the business accounts and statements are those of the entity rather than those of the proprietor, partner, investors, or other parties or groups concerned.[7]

This statement of the entity position shows clearly the tendency to carry over into a new situation the personality of the proprietor—to substitute for the proprietor the entity itself. The use of the phrase "institution in its own right," coupled with the idea that the accounts and statements are "those of the entity rather than of other parties or groups concerned," suggests that the entity notion involves much more than a mere definition of the area of attention. Indeed, in this context, entity suggests an additional personality, apart from the owners, managers, creditors, or other persons connected with the business. This implication of personality is carried on further when the entity theorist explains the assumption of continuity:

> The assumption that the business entity has continuity of life may be largely one of convenience, since no one can confidently predict the course of events. Yet some degree of continuity is the typical experience even in the midst of insolvency, liquidation, and dissolution.[8]

The personalization of the entity implied in the suggestion that the entity "has continuity of life" has good justification in that some corporate enterprises do persist over long periods of time. Actually, however, the continuity convention involves much more than mere continuance of a given corporate "person."

Accounting, like other quantitative methodologies, is based upon a set of premises as to relations between past and future events. Statements about the past do not have much significance unless they can be related to the future in some way; indeed, the basic reason for trying to interpret the past is to find guidance for the future. Continuity is, in such a context, a matter of relationships between past and future events. The continuity convention involves a great deal more than mere extension of corporate existence; certainly its meaning does not depend upon the "life" of a personalized entity. Rather, it includes assumptions such as: (*a*) that the existing pattern of economic organization (including legal rules and social attitudes) will remain unchanged; (*b*) that the operations reflected in the accounting statements will be continued in substantially the same terms as in the past—that is, that the line of products, the geographical scope of market coverage, the general patterns of sales effort, will persist; (*c*) that the economic and technological factors which are relevant to the operations will continue to exert their influence in a substantially unaltered fashion; and (*d*) that the techniques and the forms of managerial effort will be carried over into the future—that is, that there will be no change in the basic objectives, policies, or strategic plans of the management. The mere personalization of the entity and the observation that the life of such units is of some extended duration really offer but little support for the notion of continuity that is implied in accounting reports. Nor is it an adequate explanation of continuity to say that it arises because, as a consequence of modern economic activity, there has been a "transition from successive to overlapping ventures."[9]

But personalization of the entity is carried much further than this in the entity theory. The personal view of entity enters the field of valuation; personalization affects the interpretations and prescribes the very methods that may be used to establish valuations under entity theory. The entity theorist presents the following argument:

> The entity, as such, is not concerned with economic measures of valuation but rather symbolizes in terms of money various transactions reflecting a charge and discharge relationship between entity and proprietor. . . . . From the entity viewpoint, valuation at cost is natural.[10]

It is true, of course, that this position is not maintained in the face of adverse situations. For example, one writer says:

> If, for example, plant assets are acquired during a period of low prices an earning rate based upon recorded values in a later year when prices are on a much higher level is presumably less significant to actual or prospective investors or to management than a rate calculated in terms of property values revised in the light of prevailing conditions.[11]

This would indicate that the entity theorist would be willing to make adjustments in original valuations when conditions have changed to such an extent as to make this advisable; but the basic view of the entity theorist is that valuation is restricted to recording and tracing costs over the history of the enterprise.[12]

Quite apart from the merits of different bases for valuation, it is the personal aspect of the entity which justifies the cost emphasis in entity theory. Some support is found for this viewpoint, of course, in the legal personification of the corporation. Paton writes: "It is in the case of the corporation that an actual legal existence puts substance in the accountant's assumption of a business entity."[13] Yet the entity theorists are careful to point out that the entity (in these personal aspects) is a pure fiction, having no other support in fact except the legal position of the corporate unit.[14]

The difficulties in maintaining a position such as this are quite obvious. To be sure, the corporation does hold legal title to assets, and it is the contracting party with respect to business transactions; but a sole proprietor or the members of a partnership are in precisely the same position as the corporation. The entity with which accounting deals—if, indeed, it must deal with personal entities at all—is not that creature which arises from the legal formula of incorporation; the community of interest that *is* the business enterprise arises from the acts of real people and the relations among them. The existence of this community of interest depends not upon the performance of the legal rituals but upon human and economic activities. Even by the lawyers and the courts that have created and maintained the existence of corporations, the corporation is sometimes viewed as an *association of people*. Husband has already pointed out this fact; he observes that "accounting theory would probably be more realistic if it accepted as its basis the fact that the corporation is an association of flesh and blood persons who enjoy special privileges because they have complied with certain legal requirements."[15]

The personalization involved in the entity approach appears with varying degrees of emphasis in accounting literature; an example of personalization in its most extreme form is the following statement:

> Double entry is based upon the concept of duality of a single business property. This duality is created through the separation of business properties from their actual owners by placing these properties in the possession of a fictitious business entity which holds and operates such properties under an assumed trust arrangement between the business entity and the legal owners. This is purely an accounting assumption, and has no legal basis whatever. Because of this separation of the properties from the legal owners, and because of the varying legal status of these owners, it becomes necessary for the fictitious business entity to account for both the kinds of goods or things making up the property in its possession and for the kinds of ownership claims attaching to those goods.[16]

Whatever this presentation of the entity view may offer in the way of a rationalization of the double-entry mechanism, it is not a satisfying basis for a structure of accounting theory. To erect a pattern of underlying theory upon an "assumed trust arrangement" between a "fictitious business entity" and the "actual owners of property" certainly would be unrealistic, if indeed it can be defended on logical grounds at all.

Personalization of the business entity is a form of simplification which doubtless has its uses for making explanations at an elementary or tentative level; it may even serve as a means for formulating hypotheses in their rudimentary forms. Accountants of earlier times used the device of personalization—correctly or incorrectly—to present certain ideas;[17] it is still widely employed informally in discussion at various levels in many fields. But such a device cannot be the criterion for decisions as to the purpose and content of financial reports, the reason for an emphasis upon one basis of valuation over all others, or the determinant of the scope or area to which accounting processes are applied. "The conception of the business enterprise as in all cases a distinct entity or personality"[18] is not a satisfactory foundation for the integration of accounting thought.

The case against the entity position has been argued by a number of writers, some of whom have objected to the personification of business entity in no uncertain terms. Canning states:

> Imaginary entities have their proper place in the conceptual world of analysis in pure mathematics, but never in the statistical analysis of realities. Figures of speech may be useful occasionally as a device in exposition; but to hang the whole exposition of a statistical analysis and synthesis upon a figure of speech is to run the risk of conveying a memory of the figure instead of an understanding of reality.[19]

Writers have also pointed out that neither the entity nor the proprietary view actually is followed in practice. Rather, practice seems really to mix the two theories, even to the point of vacillation. Husband, for example, writes:

> Accounting principles, as frequently presented, are not entirely consistent with either the entity or the representative [proprietary] viewpoint. While the accountant subscribes fundamentally to the entity theory, he appears to shift to the representative theory when it suits his convenience.[20]

Gilman recognizes this same situation, but he argues that only inconsistency need be guarded against:

> Both the entity and the proprietary conventions have value. Like all conventions, each contains an element of artificiality. Either is valuable so long as it is consistently maintained. It is only when an unconscious shift in viewpoint from one to the other occurs that there is danger of false reasoning.[21]

Neither the proprietary theory nor the entity theory is a wholly satisfying frame of reference for accounting. Each is vulnerable in that it adopts a personality as its focus of attention. The difference between them is mostly whether the person (for whom the books are kept and to whom the reports are made) is the "proprietor" or proprietors in their human selves, or whether real people must be viewed abstractly or in the guise of a fictional entity, corporate or otherwise. The weakness in these personalized bases for accounting is that the content of accounting reports will tend to be affected by personal analogies; and issues will be decided not by considering the nature of the problems but upon some extension of personality—to reach or to support conclusions that are for the most part mere expediencies. Dependence upon personality and personal implications in accounting theory, even as a convention, does not contribute to that objectivity toward which all quantitative analysis is aimed.

In addition, it should be recognized that accounting has grown far beyond the possibility of basing its operations upon any kind of "single-valued" or general purpose theory. The uses to which accounting data are put are far too numerous to base a frame of reference upon a single personality to whom accounting reports are directed and for whom accounting records are maintained. A complete tabulation of all the purposes that accounting data are made to serve would probably be as useless as it would be complex; the number of parties at interest is not small, and the functions that accounting data are to serve overlap considerably between various parties at interest. But it is possible to discern at least three broad areas in which accounting figures and reports have different kinds of significance. It is worth while considering these to make the point clear.

The most direct demands upon accounting records and reports are made by management, for it is management that determines the scope of that procedural system which underlies the accounting process itself. In this sphere the accounting system is a device for facilitating the managerial process, quite apart from the production of over-all financial reports. The accounting system is relied upon to serve as a memorandum or recording device, to preserve minutiae of business events, and to collate related facts in systematic fashion—as in the case of customer and creditor accounting; here, accounting records preserve numerous details concerning credit extensions and reimbursements. In addition to this, accounting procedures provide a part of the system of communication that is so important an element in organization; accounting reports are one means of simplifying the problem of management from the standpoints of observation, evaluation, and control. The routines of accounting are nearly always integrated with the over-all system of internal check and administrative organization. Still further, accounting data in special forms and combinations are employed by management to aid in the solution of problems of policy, strategy, or procedure. From all these angles, the accounting system is a part of the management system; the data that management needs and insists upon from the accounting department are not of the sort that can be established from a single-valued theory of accounting, even if management were the only group to be served.

Another group of parties at interest, with special needs and desires in the way of accounting data, may be broadly described as social control agencies. Various governmental units rely upon special forms of accounting summaries to implement taxation, to regulate prices and production, to control the issuance and marketing of securities, to protect creditors and others from the effects of excessive or restrictive practices with respect to dividends, to deal with "unfair" competitive or labor practices, or to arbitrate disputes that affect the public interest. Trade and other voluntary associations employ accounting data to study and interpret developments within sundry industries. Economists and statisticians employ accounting data for various analyses, of importance in both academic and practical fields; nearly all studies of business are based to some extent upon information provided by accounting records and reports. This area of use for accounting data is indeed large; there are many kinds of questions to be answered and many contexts in which they arise.

There is still a third broad channel through which accounting data are run for specific purposes. This may be described as the over-all process of credit extension and investment. Not only present owners and creditors but also prospective lenders or investors rely upon accounting reports to furnish information which bears upon the questions they must face and the decisions that they must make. The kinds of data that are useful in establishing a line of credit over short time periods, moreover, are not the same as those needed for long-term investment decisions; and there are numerous special uses for the information service provided by accounting records and reports. All these needs cannot be met by a general-purpose, oversimplified structure of accounting theory based upon simple notions of proprietorship or entity.

These three broad areas of use for accounting data are sufficiently different to indicate that no single personality could possibly maintain all the various points of view and attitudes that are involved. The uses of accounting information are manifold, and the single-person approach must either emphasize some part of these to the exclusion of others, or it must compromise them all. There is need for a more objective and more fundamental approach to the problems of accounting theory than is offered by either the proprietary or the entity basis, if only because the manifold uses of accounting data cannot be reconciled with a personalistic approach.

However, there is still another reason for seeking a new approach to accounting theory—one that is perhaps more powerful than any of those thus far given. Both the entity and the proprietary concepts actually break down when they are applied to specific situations. When corporations raise their capital from various sources, such as bank loans, debenture and mortgage bonds, various kinds of preferred and classified common stock, the notion of proprietorship is not very clear. The differences between certain classes of securities are not always easy to establish; it is not always a simple matter to decide just where creditor relations cease and proprietary equities begin. Many securities which are called "bonds" have some of the attributes of stock, and vice versa; conversion privileges, cumulative features, and participation clauses tend to make somewhat vague the distinctions that might otherwise be established. Thus, the concept of proprietorship is not one that lends itself well to objective application.

Although the entity notion avoids the issue of making fine distinctions between debts and proprietary claims—by putting a fictitious person between the operations and the parties at interest—it still runs into difficulties when it is applied to practice. Despite the support of legal notions about corporations, the reality of corporate administration involves a separation of management from ownership. The corporate body is only an outward evidence of a difference in organization which has somewhat far-reaching consequences. Corporate management tends to become in practice an intermediary between the operations that are carried on and the owners; but by extension this in turn evolves into another situation in which management becomes a clearinghouse or administrative agency through which are bent together in a common effort the different interests of owners, long-term and short-term creditors, current suppliers of services or goods, governmental or other social control forces, employees, and even competitors and affiliates. In this situation management is indeed far removed from the application of neat theories of authority delegations following the lines of property rights; management is not the servant of the proprietors but rather the conciliatory agency between two or among several of these groups. Special instances of creditor control, employee representation, government supervision, or industry co-operation illustrate the point; what, in cases such as these, is the significance of the corporate entity? Viewed realistically, the corporation is a conglomeration of personalities, resources, conditions, and relationships; and this conglomeration is but faintly if at all recognized in the legal fiction of the corporate "person." In this framework wages are not merely costs of production; they are at the same time a distributive share of the general proceeds from operations; interest and dividends are other shares in the same set of proceeds; the distinctions between "cost" and "distribution of income" are no longer so sharp as they might have appeared under other circumstances.

The shifts between entity and proprietary viewpoints that are characteristic of accounting practice have already been pointed out; but it should now be clear that these shifts do not originate from mere carelessness or perversity. This shifting viewpoint really comes into existence because neither proprietary nor entity theory meets all the needs, fits all the facts, or allows for the exigencies of solving practical problems. The result is not merely faulty reasoning in some cases; the procedures that tend to be established by the peculiar admixtures of differing points of view are sometimes arbitrary in the extreme, and they unquestionably must appear awkward and confusing to the lay mind.

Again, with particular reference to the entity theory, the notion of business entity is not clear as to how it is actually applied; the corporate person, from which the justification for the entity approach is presumed to be derived, does not always coincide with the practical notions of entity that are found in practice. The entity theorists recognize this themselves, as exemplified in the following:

> In some instances a department or other section of a business may become of sufficient importance to justify treatment for certain purposes as a subordinate form of entity. In other instances, a number of distinct corporations may be so closely related as to justify treatment of the group, for certain purposes, as one corporate enterprise.[22]

The point is that a business unit is not a thing that can be defined universally and with rigid precision—certainly the corporate charter does not define a business unit in more than a legalistic sense. All business units are but parts of a greater whole; vice versa, most business units are themselves but combinations of smaller units. A thing or situation which may be a most useful and workable unit of business from one point of view is likely to prove awkward and unsuited to other uses and conditions. In the last analysis the notion of a unit of business is but a means of specifying the area of attention—a delimited and prescribed set of activities which give rise to the kinds of data with which accounting is to deal. Some such unit must serve as the basis for accounting; but it must be a unit devoid of personal implications and at the same time sufficiently definite to make clear just where its boundaries lie; it must be one that may be applied to various forms of organization and different kinds of activities; and it must be one that has definite relation to the processes and the results that accounting is expected to achieve. Such a unit is to be found in the concept of a fund.

Immediately, however, there arises an issue of terminology; there are at least three separate meanings attached to the word "fund." Like a great many other terms employed in accounting, this one seems to reflect the looseness of language that is commonly observed in business; from this the accountant cannot escape entirely, no matter how hard he may try. But here it is imperative that these ambiguities be resolved and that the fund concept be clearly stated. The first step in this process is to review the various meanings which have been given to "fund" or "funds."

In its simplest connotation—which also seems to be the loosest and most confusing usage—"fund" or "funds" is synonymous with "cash resources." This is apparent in those too frequently encountered expressions that serve crudely to describe certain financial aspects of business: specifically, such phrases as "raising funds" or "being without funds." This use of the word probably originated from attempts at euphemism when reference was made to events and transactions "tainted" with monetary significance; but whatever its origin, this use of "fund" adds nothing to the language of accounting except a possible alternative to "cash" or "money." Yet even this is not exactly true, for, when "funds" are referred to in this sense, the reference is nearly always too vague and too indefinite to permit the substitution of "cash" or "money." One never hears of a "funds" account or a "fund" transaction, although cash accounts and cash transactions are commonly encountered. The use of "funds" to substitute for "cash" is loose and superficial, and it really should be discouraged.

A second meaning of "fund"—one of more real significance—is that which appears in industrial and commercial accounting in the context of "funds and reserves." A typical illustration of this usage is the sinking fund. The sinking fund is but rarely a mere aggregation of cash; usually it is best described as a collection of resources assembled in some more or less systematic fashion, usually for the purpose of retiring long-term debt. The really central notion in a sinking fund is the grouping or segregation of certain types of financial assets for a special end; the combination of periodic deposits with aggregations of income is computed to retire certain indebtedness over some fixed period of time. Of course, there are variants that depart somewhat from this notion; however, as a generic concept, a sinking fund is an *invested* fund, i.e., there is involved not only a segregation of assets but also a separate set of "income-producing" operations. The element of income production distinguishes a sinking fund from the category of cash resources because cash of and by itself can produce no income in the accounting sense. Investment, conversion, or exchange—singly or in combination—are important parts of every notion of income that accountants have been willing to accept.

As a matter of fact, sinking-fund accounts include specific classifications for investment items (usually, though not necessarily, of marketable character) in addition to cash balances. Moreover, such groups of accounts usually include classifications for certain items of revenue and expense to record the effects of the operations within the fund. Sometimes—perhaps too frequently—the revenue and expense aspects of the sinking fund are reflected in the general financial reports only as offsets to the interest charges on the debt to be extinguished; or they may be lumped together as a single item among "extraneous" or "financial" items in the general statement of income. In this connection it is worth noting that the sinking fund may, or may not, be a part of the assets that are under the direct control of the general management; the incidence of control is evidently not the exclusive criterion as to the separate maintenance of the sinking-fund accounts.

Although most discussions of sinking-fund accounts include some mention of a "reserve" for sinking fund, this reserve is neither a part of the sinking fund itself nor does it necessarily have any direct relation to the operations of the fund. There may be a fund without a reserve, a reserve without a fund, or both a fund and a reserve of equal or dissimilar amounts. The usual practice is to treat the reserve account as an "earmarked" surplus item, usually established by transfer from earned surplus as provided in bond indentures or preferred-stock agreements.

In this sense of "fund" there are involved (1) a segregation of assets for a given purpose and (2) a partial recognition of the set of separate operations which pertain to those assets. This idea has found expression in accounting textbooks in the following general pattern of definition: "A fund account is an asset account; it represents cash, securities, or other assets set aside for a specific purpose."[23]

A slight extension of this meaning is the third notion of "fund" which is used in accounting, one which has particular interest for the present discussion.[24] A fund, in the context of accounting for government and eleemosynary institutions, is a unit of operations or a center of interest; and, in a completely nonpersonal sense, the fund is the accounting entity. In these areas of accounting, funds of various kinds are established to separate those elements of administrative organization, particular activities, or special purposes that may be important, and the double-entry mechanism of bookkeeping is applied to each unit separately.

In "fund" accounting a fund is not mere cash resources, and it is more than a mere collection of assets set aside for a particular purpose. The accounts of each fund recognize not only all the asset items but also all the equities that pertain to that fund; in addition, there are also present complete classifications of revenue, expense, and income accounts. These, taken together, provide a general ledger trial balance complete in all respects as to the operations covered by the definition of the fund. In theory at least, this trial balance arises from a separate set of books kept for each fund; each of the separate sets of books might encompass any desired amount of subsidiary ledgers, chronological records, vouchers and business papers, and system procedures; each fund ledger would be comparable to a conventional set of books for a commercial or industrial firm.

It is possible, of course, to maintain the segregation of funds without actually operating separate systems of accounts for the individual units. The accounting procedures may, if desired, be centralized completely for all the funds of a given institution; but, even then, the reports are kept separate, and the accounting classifications are such as to make possible the reporting of operations as if each fund did in fact have its own accounting system. There is here a basic notion of some importance; in governmental and institutional accounting the fund is the *unit* of accounting in the sense that it represents the field of attention covered by a given set of financial records and reports.

The notion of a fund has not been encumbered by personalistic thinking; it is free from those extensions of meaning which frequently creep into a theory based upon personalizations. And it is not bound up with attitudes about valuation, the form and content of financial reports, and related matters. There is real advantage to be gained from an approach that makes it possible to consider the problem of accounting from a fresh point of view—one which facilitates the separation of issues now hopelessly bound together in the personalistic systems of thought exemplified by both proprietary and entity theories.

The notion of a fund as applied to commercial and industrial accounting is not really so far-fetched as it may seem. As we shall see, there are many instances of its application even in extant practice. Hord, in an article that emphasizes an entity approach to a problem of valuation, states: "Since the properties are held in common for all the different owners so that there can be no identification of particular ownership claims with particular goods or things on hand, the reporting must be done as if the entire business properties constituted *one great fund* for which an accounting must be made."[25] Paton makes a similar statement: "There is but *one underlying fund of values*. This fund, however, has two statistical descriptions, each of decided importance in the affairs of the enterprise."[26]

We are not here concerned with the mere chance mention of a word in these quotations; there is additional evidence of the fact that the notion of fund entity is applied in extant practice, and this evidence will be presented in chapter iv. But, before this material can be examined, there is good reason to make an extended analysis of the concepts which apply to and evolve from the fund approach. Chapters ii and iii are devoted to this task. Although the titles of these chapters suggest that they are aimed at terminological problems, their real purpose is to establish some of the major premises of fund theory; this should precede any attempt to apply or even to observe elements of the fund theory in operation. Chapters v and vi have to do with some of the broad questions of financial reporting and some of the problems that exist in this field, against which the fund theory may offer some useful means of attack. In chapter vii appears a summary presentation of the fund theory as applied to an extended illustration, in which will appear some interesting possibilities for new forms of financial reports. The reader who may desire a preliminary view of the ends toward which this study is directed may wish to examine chapter vii before reading the theoretical exposition. To the writer, however, it has seemed more desirable to present the subject of fund theory in the way it developed from the process of study; therefore, the operational notions which give the fund theory a meaningful content will be analyzed before any attempt is made to suggest the ways in which that theory may be applied.

CHAPTER II

FUND TERMINOLOGY: ASSETS AND EQUITIES

The fund theory begins with a delimitation of the area of attention to which accounting records and reports are oriented. This, as has been stated, is a matter of abstracting from the whole field of financial and managerial operations those segments of activity which can be dealt with as accounting units, here referred to as funds. There are certain advantages in starting from such a premise; at least, setting up the fund concept as the central notion for an integration of accounting theory does not preclude the separate analysis and development of those issues that arise in completing the frame of reference. The approach that has been adopted makes it possible to consider the problem of terminology in broad and general outlines, quite apart from those personal implications that condition both the proprietary and the entity approach. This chapter is concerned with basic elements of accounting terminology—the system of operational concepts which serve to implement and give meaning to the fund theory.

Terminology is not merely a matter of etymology and definition; it has a much broader function than merely to state the meaning of words. Terminology is a problem of *language*—it is a *system* of words that describes the relationships between concepts, so that (1) ideas can be communicated and (2) structures of thought and action can be built up from these relationships. The aims of terminology set certain restrictions upon its content, the first of which is that the language as developed must be such as will permit the transmission of individual observations from one person to another in clear and unequivocal fashion. We know and can understand only that which we have experienced, and ideas can be communicated only through the channels of things that we have done or can do. That is, the terms that are to be employed in the communication of ideas must have operational content.[1]

To make clear what is encompassed by the notion of operational content, consider the following definition of an asset: "An asset may be defined as any consideration, material or otherwise, which is owned by a business enterprise (or in which the enterprise has an equitable interest) and which has a value to that enterprise."[2]

This is a descriptive definition. It serves in a general way to indicate what an asset might be; it relates the accounting notion of asset to ideas of ownership, equitable interest, business enterprise, and value—ideas of other fields to which accounting is related. But quite apart from the merits of the definition on other grounds, it is not operational in content; it does not specify the things that must be done to establish the presence or the absence of an asset, and it does not clearly mark out what tests are to be applied in distinguishing assets from other things. The meaning of this definition depends upon a number of things that are not specified within it. What operations are involved in recognizing a "consideration," in establishing the existence of ownership or equitable interest, and in measuring the value to the business enterprise?

By contrast, the "unamortized cost" definition of an asset approaches more closely the standard of operational content. According to this view, assets are

> those factors acquired for production which have not reached the point in the business process where they may be treated as "cost of sales" or "expense." . . . . Under this usage, assets or costs incurred would clearly mean charges awaiting future revenue, whereas expenses or costs applied would mean charges against present revenue.[3]

This definition is oriented to the operations of accounting, and assets are described in terms of those operations. Under certain circumstances, and with the further specification of the processes of amortization and accrual, the definition would relate the notion of assets to the accounting process in a way that could not fail to be precise in its meaning. The requirement of operational content avoids ambiguity by specifying the concept in terms of the particular operations that are to be performed.[4]

The mere communication of ideas, however, is only one of the aims of terminology; there is also involved the integration of structures of thought from the relationships that are expressed by the terms which are employed. This second aim places another restriction upon the terminological pattern. This is that there must be some pervasive uniformity or some homogeneity of substance which threads through the entire system of terminology, preserving the relationships between terms in some underlying fashion. In the physical sciences this is achieved by relating concepts to basic notions of mass, space, and time. The continuity of thought in these fields is preserved by the fact that these basic ideas are the underlying means of expression of all the relationships with which scientific terminology is concerned.[5] Perhaps the meaning of this requirement for terminology may be made more clear by further reference to the definition of an asset that has just been presented.

The definition of an asset in terms of unamortized cost does have operational content; but the definition is unsatisfactory from the point of view of homogeneity of substance. The definition of an asset in terms of unamortized cost is weak in that it does not include all the things that are commonly regarded as assets; further, it does not specify the underlying thread of relationships—the basic uniformity of substance—with which assets and related terms are concerned. Financial claims (cash, bank deposits, and receivables) are certainly assets—at least they are so regarded in practice—but they are not *costs*, however closely they may be related to the concepts of "measured consideration" or "historical price aggregates" cited as criteria of costs by the framers of the definition. Financial claims cannot as such be fitted into the pattern of amortization which is suggested by the definition of assets; they are not "charges awaiting future revenue" or "charges against present revenue." The trouble with the definition is that the operations specified are not broadly enough conceived to encompass all the activities in which assets are involved, so as to include in a homogeneous pattern all the items that are brought together in the definition. If financial claims are to be excluded from the category of assets, the definition is satisfactory to prescribe the meaning of the word; but it still fails in the sense that the relationship between financial claims and assets is not indicated. Even though the definition be amended to include financial claims, under the argument that financial claims "reflect the bargained prices arising in preceding transactions and consequently bear a similarity to technical cost factors,"[6] the unamortized cost definition cannot be applied to things that are not costs and which are not subject to amortization.

The importance of homogeneity of substance can be seen even more clearly when a terminological structure is considered as a whole. In quantitative philosophy it is the *relationships* between phenomena that are of prime importance. From this point of view, the real significance of assets is the relation between the asset notion and other ideas, such as expense, equities, revenue, income, and the like. Unless there is some fundamental pattern of relationships, recognized in terms of some underlying principle or phenomenon, these terms can have little meaning in the larger sense, no matter how precisely their operational content is specified. What is needed to provide a useful terminology for the integration of theory is some notion or set of ideas comparable to the physical ones of mass, space, and time. Is there such a basis for a system of accounting terminology?

An approach to the problem of defining accounting concepts from the point of view of homogeneity of substance may be made by observing that the aim of all economic (or financial) activity is *want satisfaction*—"a change of state in an economic subject, produced and maintained over some period of time by an economic agency."[7] Wants are satisfied by the conversion or transformation of services released from (rendered by) economic agencies, such as persons or things. Thus the underlying material of economics is the aggregation of services devoted to want satisfaction through the processes of storage, transformation, and exchange. By means of these processes services are built into various forms and are released to various individuals or activities. Wealth is thus an aggregation of service potentials, and the business system is a mechanism to promote the separation, combination, transfer, or other metamorphosis proceeding toward the satisfaction of wants, as they are finally expressed in various market situations. Commodities, productive agencies, money and other financial claims; special advantages, opportunities, or capabilities have thus a common significance —they are service potentials, capable of satisfying wants through the processes of business.

Service potentials are not to be confused with utility. Utility includes the reaction of some human being to a given economic situation, and the utility of a thing is quite likely to be different for each person exposed to it.[8] Nor are economic services to be confused with "value," "price," or "cost." These terms are extensions of the service concept; they bring into play various kinds of appraisals of expected service conversions with respect to available alternatives. Value, price, or cost may be employed to quantify or to measure[9] service potentials, but they are derivatives of the service concept, not synonymous with it.

The notion of economic services and service potentials is not entirely new in accounting literature. Paton and Littleton give clear recognition to this:

> Accounting uses money-price only because it is a convenient common denominator. . . . . It is not "money" that is significant; it is not "price" that is significant. "Service" is the significant element behind the accounts, that is, service-potentialities, which, when exchanged, bring still other service-potentialities into the enterprise.
>
> Behind accounting's array of figures, which laymen may think represent values or money, or, at best, price, lie the tangible and intangible embodiments of services.[10]

Canning made the following statement:

> If the necessary service in question is to be procured through control of the agent rendering it (e.g., a machine), a valuation of the agent may be found. The agent is worth no more and no less than (1) the present worth of future outlays necessary to obtain like services in like amounts by the *best available alternative means*, less (2) the present worth of future outlays necessary to obtain the agent's future service in the *most economical manner*. But it is the assured, separable service-series, not the agent rendering them, that constitutes the essence of enterprise assets.[11]

But the application of the service basis to accounting terminology has not been carried as far as it might have been.

ASSETS

Contrary to most popular notions, assets are in essence neither physical, legal, nor even financial phenomena. It may at times be convenient to talk of assets as if they were physical, legal, or financial things; but this convenience is achieved at the expense of exactness of expression. The material or physical notion of an asset is denied by the fact that choses-in-action, leaseholds, franchises, air rights, and prepayments are all perfectly good assets. Redressable rights do not express the essential nature of assets, for legal title is not the determinant of asset existence.[12] Mortgaged property is shown among the assets, despite the fact that title is passed (though conditionally) to the mortgagee, and the person who controls the fund in which the property is listed as an asset holds nothing more than the equity of redemption. Deferred charges for leasehold improvements, relocation of machinery, and extensive development campaigns involving research and advertising are certainly not evidenced by legal titles, though they may be perfectly good assets. The accruals that may appear on the balance sheet under the asset caption are seldom evidenced by legal rights which correspond to the amounts shown.

Assets are not monetary or financial in significance, for transactions that do not involve money may result in the recognition of assets (as in the case of exchanges of property for other property, gifts, and accretions); further, money itself has asset significance only to the extent that it may be used to acquire something else or in that it serves to postpone such acquisitions to some future time. Although assets are measured in monetary units, the nature of assets is not directly related to any monetary notion, any more than a bag of sugar is a hundred "pounds" or a farm is eighty "acres." Assets are economic in nature; they are embodiments of future want satisfaction in the form of service potentials that may be transformed, exchanged, or stored against future events. Whatever means or method is employed to measure assets (cost, price, appraisal, or arbitrary valuation), assets are service potentials, not physical things, legal rights, or money claims.

This service concept of assets lends itself well to the processes of amortization and accrual and eliminates the need for the conventional assumption that "costs attach."[13] Labor services applied directly to physical or intangible product need not be viewed as being physically connected with that product to justify an accretion of the asset goods in process.[14] Accounting for fixed assets under the service-potential notion is clearly seen not to be a matter of reproduction of the asset or replacement at the end of its life-period; nor is it, necessarily, the mere amortization of historical cost. Rather, it is a matter of measuring service conversions or releases, as these relate to the operations that are carried on. The services embodied in a fixed asset may be dissipated, even though its outward appearance remains unchanged; its economic content may decrease as services are applied, are diverted to unintended uses, as they change in significance, or evanesce in nonuse.

It may be objected that service is a protean concept—that it has as many meanings as there are different situations in which it is employed. The significance of services depends upon the individual who may control their use and upon the plans, situations, or aspirations with which they may become involved. Removing the personal aspects of the entity (which we have insisted upon) may seem to make the problem of recognizing and measuring service potentialities impossible to solve. Things are not always the same when viewed from different angles; does not the personalistic view serve as a basis for making relevant interpretations? For example, the service attributes of the same five-ton motor truck would seem to be quite different in (*a*) the inventory of a seller of used motor vehicles and in (*b*) the garage of a retail coal dealer—if only because the alternatives open to these two individuals as to the truck are not the same. The service significance of the asset would seem to depend upon whose truck it is!

The answer to this is that it is not the person of the owner or the manager of the business which affects the interpretation of service attributes; rather it is the *operation* (the fund activity) which determines the service significance of the asset. And, even *within* the area of property control or management that we call the business firm, there may be different aspects of service potentials that ought to be considered; further, there may even be different *valuations* for certain items, depending upon the fund activities involved in the particular case. The service concept is no more protean than the notions of "cost"[15] or "value"[16]—which notions are the only bases as yet proposed to express the meaning of assets in accounting.

The service concept of assets is operational in the strictest sense; quite apart from the financial means of expressing and carrying on business transactions, every accounting unit is aimed at the fulfilment of some purpose, for which the services embodied in assets are of importance. The acquisition, holding, conversion, and delivery of these services to the various parties at interest *is* the operation of the unit. Therefore, the services embodied in asset forms are the essence of asset definition. The problem of measurement is, of course, important; but the frame of reference must be established in the first instance on grounds of operational significance and homogeneity of substance. For theory to be more than a rationalization of practice, it is essential that the exigencies of measurement should not color the pattern of thought.

The service concept of assets is the central idea in the terminology of the fund theory. Basically, a fund is a collection of service potentials that have been brought together for some functional purpose—administrative, entrepreneurial, or social. The other aspects of accounting terminology must be related to the asset notion if the structure as a whole is to have homogeneity of substance.

EQUITIES

The entity theorist's view of equities is that these are "claims against the assets"; the proprietary theorist would insist that they are obligations of the proprietor (liabilities) *and* the ownership rights of the proprietor (net worth). For the fund theory both of these views are rejected; equities are viewed rather as restrictions that apply to assets in the fund, which therefore condition the operations of the fund as dictated by the management. It is important to consider the reasons for adopting this view.

Claims do not arise against assets but against persons; if attention is focused upon the operations of the fund of assets, the property rights do not have much substance. Assets are used to satisfy claims (indeed, the courts frequently "attach" assets for this purpose), but the claims lie in the field of property rights, not in property itself. This is partially evidenced by the fact that creditors never have specific claims against particular assets; even mortgage-holders do not have more than priority of payment from the proceeds of a foreclosure sale of the particular asset. But there is more reason for the denial of legal significance of equities than this.

Characteristically, the items that are displayed on the right side of the balance sheet as "liabilities" represent future obligations; otherwise, liabilities are but past-due indebtedness. But the legal obligation to pay does not obtain until the due dates of these obligations; thus, that which is shown on the balance sheet as an equity is an *anticipated* legal liability, not a real one. The difference between the legal notion of obligation to pay and the accounting notion of "equity" is seen in the case of accrued items, such as interest, salaries and wages, taxes, etc.; these do not show the present obligation to pay for services rendered but rather show an attempt to forecast what the legal liabilities will be, on the basis of events that have occurred. Redressable rights arise only on the payment dates specified in the relevant contracts; even then, those rights do not operate upon the assets, but upon legal personalities in the capacity of proprietor, owner, or manager. The continuity convention implies that debts will be paid as they mature, and the accounting notion of equity is a recognition of this fact, over and above the extant legal obligations that are the supposed basis for equity presentation.

This is even more evident in the notions that attach to the various aspects of proprietary equity (capital stock and various kinds of surplus and reserves). The claim of the stockholder, whenever it does come into the field of legal significance, is not fundamentally different with respect to the items classified as capital stock, capital surplus, appropriated or unappropriated earned surplus. Indeed, appropriations of surplus arise primarily from managerial or directorial decision rather than from any legal considerations. The principal objective that is aimed at in the classification of proprietary equities is to give expression to the various kinds of restrictions imposed upon the use of the assets, not to show their legal significance. Reserves for anticipated losses, for contingencies, for maintenance of working capital, or for extension of plant are not "legal" but restrictive appropriations of surplus, based upon the decisions of those who exercise discretion and prudence in the over-all management of the firm.

The case is made even stronger by the fact that there are some equities which defy classification as between "proprietary" and "liability" categories; e.g., reserves for self-insurance and other "expense-equalization" reserves.[17] In such cases the equities are not evidenced by any present or future redressable rights arising from contract, yet they are not unqualified proprietary claims in any but a momentary sense. The real significance of equities of this character is to be found in the restrictions they impose upon the asset fund, not the quasi-legal or equitable considerations that may be involved.

Still another aspect of the significance of equities merits consideration here. If the terminology of accounting that describes the right-hand items as they are shown on balance sheets is valid at all, it should apply to each of the various situations that must be met by such terminology—i.e., it should apply to any and all items that the accountant shows on the "equity" side of his balance sheet. In the case of government or eleemosynary accounts, the right side of the balance sheet includes items that do not ordinarily appear on the books of financial or industrial concerns, such as "Reserve for Encumbrances," "Appropriations,"[18] and the like. These accounts, and similar ones employed in institutional accounting, are conceived of as restrictions on the asset fund, not in any legal or equitable sense of claims against assets or persons.

Moreover, the restrictions or reservations represented by equities do not apply to transformations or exchanges, nor do they limit (as a general rule) asset items to specific uses. All that is required to maintain and support (i.e., "balance") an equity is for sufficient assets to be retained within the area of operations and subject to the control of the management, so that they are available for the satisfaction of redressable rights if and when those rights arise. The nature of accounting equities is clearly seen to be that of restrictions applicable to the assets in the fund.

RESIDUAL EQUITY AND THE DOUBLE-ENTRY PRINCIPLE

The basic mechanism of double-entry bookkeeping has been justified on various grounds. The proprietary theorist would establish it on the reasoning that the fund of assets "belongs to" the proprietor, after his indebtedness to outsiders has been taken into consideration.[19] The basic equation is thus "property, less debts, equals net worth." The entity theorist would insist that the equation should be "property equals claims to property,"[20] and some would go so far as to postulate a duality of property to establish this notion.[21]

The basis for the equality of assets and equities is to be found in the notion of residual equity—a final and pervasive restriction upon fund assets or any residual thereof, in the sense that the entire asset fund is confined to the set of operations for which the fund is established. This has support in the legal position of the proprietor or the common stockholder as regards priority of rights and residual claims; the residual owner stands the losses and reaps the gains after contractual rights of the other interested parties have been satisfied. But it is the notion of residual equity that establishes the equality of assets and equities, not a duality of property, or a notion that "property must be owned by someone." The equation underlying the double-entry mechanism is, from the fund point of view, "assets equal restrictions upon assets"; it arises from the concept of residual equity (or "fund equity") as a fact of business and social organization.

SUMMARY

Accounting terminology is a system of words or a language in which two requirements must be met: operational content and homogeneity of substance. The basic notion in all accounting terminology is the concept of service potentials, and the asset notion is the simplest expression of this. Quite apart from the problem of measurement that is involved in stating the amounts of assets in dollar terms, the service concept is the basis of asset significance. As we shall see, this is precisely what is involved in describing expense, revenue, or kindred concepts. The equity notion, however, is not to be taken as an accounting for assets in terms of their ownership, nor is it a matter of stating claims against the assets; rather, equities are viewed as restrictions upon the assets in a fund. The implications of this will be apparent in the discussion of expense and revenue to be undertaken in the following chapter.

CHAPTER III

FUND TERMINOLOGY: EXPENSE, REVENUE, AND INCOME

THUS far there have been established three basic notions that underlie the fund theory of accounting. First, there was adopted as a starting-point the idea that the fund was a means of limiting the area of attention by defining the group of activities or operations with which any one set of accounting records is concerned; second, it was pointed out that the basic requirements of terminology—operational content and homogeneity of substance—required the definition of assets in terms of economic services. Quite apart from the methods that may be employed to measure assets in quantitative terms, and the problems of valuation that are bound up with the choice between such methods, assets are service potentials rather than legal rights, costs, or physical things. Similarly, it has been pointed out that equities are restrictions that apply to the assets that are present in a given fund; equities are not legal liabilities, equitable claims, or ownership rights.

These notions are important with respect to the terminological significance of expense and revenue; it is proposed in this chapter to relate the expense and the revenue concepts to the three basic premises already presented. There will be some occasion to consider the meaning and the limitations of income as an accounting concept, especially with reference to the parties at interest and the functions that accounting data are made to serve. This chapter thus completes the bare outlines of the fund theory, in that the more important relationships and terms are covered; the applications of such ideas and the implications of the fund theory in specific connections may then be considered.

EXPENSE

Services are put into a fund for a specific purpose, not to remain there undisturbed for an indefinite period, but to be directed at the objectives specified in the purpose of the fund. The operations of the fund—regardless of what the purpose of such operations may be—involves the conversion and ultimate release of the impounded services through certain channels; expense is simply the draining-off or the release of converted services into those channels during some period of time. Ideally, the release of services is the volitional act of the person who manages the fund; in addition, the ideal situation would imply that the services are released solely and completely to the channels or objectives that embody the purpose for which the fund was created. This corresponds to the extant notion that expense is the "cost of producing revenue"; but it is broader than just that. The service concept of expense as a release of service to the designated objectives of the fund applies not only to profit-seeking activities but also to service operations without any motivation for gain—indeed, it applies even when there is no hope of revenue. An accounting concept should fit all the situations to which it is applied, and the notion of expense is no exception.

The difficult part of the expense problem lies in the fact that the releases of service may be largely nonvolitional, uncontrollable, or even automatic; and the services may be released to channels other than those that ideally would be chosen for their disposition. The expenditures of service are not all revenue-producing; some may spill outside the intended trough. In one sense these facts result from the imperfections of human behavior, in that we do not know how to control service flows—or that, if we do know, we are not able to carry out the intention because of the imperfections of administration and organization. Still another side of this problem is that, however much we might prefer them to be otherwise, services are joint in their ultimate significance; that is, services simply do not occur in discrete bundles that can be kept entirely separate and traced with precision, except in a very small number of transactions. There is something to be gained from a careful examination of this last angle of the situation.

JOINT SERVICES

The joint nature of services is evident even at the point of their acquisition. The process of production is an assimilation of various kinds of services into new combinations; the operations of trading as well as manufacturing businesses are but conversions of services acquired from one set of exchanges into new forms represented by tangible or intangible products that are again exchanged or devoted to final ends. The services thus brought together are not merely contributory to the product; they are also *complementary* to each other. Services are often required because other services have already been acquired; one item frequently trails others along with it, either concomitantly or in sequence. There is no point in hiring workers unless tools and materials are available; unless sheltered working space (heated, lighted, and ventilated), power supply, storerooms, inspection and maintenance crews and facilities, and supervisory and administrative staff are also provided. The combination of resources inherent to carrying on those operations for which a fund of assets is created has the effect of making service capacities joint at the initial stage of acquisition.

Then, too, the amount and the kind of service required in the form of one factor of production are affected by alterations in the service available from or required of another—stemming from variations in quality, efficiency, or other variables in the composite picture. The labor required for a given operation may be increased or decreased by alterations in the quality or the specifications of materials; by differences in machine setup or speed; by shifts in the policy or in the efficiency of operations with respect to maintenance; by changes in the intensiveness of inspection, or variations in the degree of quality to be maintained; and, also, by differences in the intelligence and alertness of supervisors, administrators, and workers in their various capacities. Services are jointly related in that there are a number of closely interwoven patterns that exist between them, and these may have different effects under varying conditions.

The problem of joint relations applies also to the other end of the fund operation. Specific channels through which services are released are never so well defined as they are assumed to be. The phenomenon of joint products is not confined to extractive or analytical industry in the physical sense; practically every "product" of every fund is made up of a number of components, that is, a product is often a conglomeration of joint effects. The "product" of a railroad is, "obviously," transportation; but this involves freight and passenger traffic over various geographic areas and includes different kinds of accommodations and results. Passenger traffic itself is not a simple product but a peculiar combination of convenience, time and space dimensions, comfort, entertainment, and perhaps other things. The very complexity of the results that ensue from fund operations makes it impossible to be sure that services do in fact reach the channels into which a final attainment of the aims of the fund would require them to go. The attempt to separate services that fail to reach the designated goal from those which do reach it is foredoomed to failure in the practical world; the shots which reach the target seldom can be told apart from those that miss.

It is not by mere chance that expense is presented in financial statements as applying to a time period; any attempt to trace all joint services through to the end of a single transaction or the attainment of specific aims is but a futile gesture. The only feasible working concept of expense is a *flow* through time of services released to eventual ends from the fund of assets under consideration; it is a thing that cannot be measured "by the transaction," because of the joint-service phenomenon. Although it is true that services are converted and released through the medium of transactions, many of these transactions are of such continuous and nonvisible nature and of such complex makeup that the transaction concept of expense must fail. Despite the effort of the cost accountant to trace the effects of joint services to specific sales and deliveries, the result can never be attained in any theoretically acceptable sense, however useful these operations may be in practice.[1]

There may be, of course, various "classifications" of expense, and items may be segregated for various purposes in any desired fashion; thus, it is possible to present in financial statements as many classes of expense as desired. But the expense concept is not a transaction concept; expense is a flow through time of services released from a fund of assets to specific purposes or to other areas of control. Even then there are still implications of joint service; depreciation charges, financing costs, and a host of other items raise problems of measurement even with respect to time periods. However, the assignment of such charges to periods of time is less difficult, relatively, than to attempt to trace them to particular transactions.[2]

REVENUE

This term, or whatever synonym is employed in practice (such as gross receipts, income), stands for a concept difficult to define descriptively. Some of the extant definitions are quite cumbersome, as, for example:

> *Revenue is the aggregate of all decreases in asset and cost factors attributable to the volume of business in question, and the addition to equities (income) which arises out of the fact that the proceeds of sale—assuming operations to be successful—exceed the expirations involved.* In all those cases where the costs of revenue exceed the new asset values accruing from sales the revenue figure evidently represents only the portion of the costs or expenses equivalent to such new values.[3]

The fact that defining revenue is a problem of distinguishing it from other sources of service potentials is shown in another definition (of "income"—in this context, synonymous with revenue) as follows:

> Income is an increase in wealth, provided it be understood that it does not include an increase in wealth resulting from gift, appreciation (meaning thereby an increase in the market

value of an asset or an increase in its cost of reproduction or replacement), or investment (as in the case of a stockholder's contribution to the capital of a corporation).[4]

This phase of the situation is met by Paton and Littleton through the following notion: "The revenue of the enterprise is represented, finally, by the flow of funds from customers or patrons in exchange for the product of the business, either commodities or services."[5]

The fundamental operation encompassed by the revenue concept is obviously the contribution of assets to the fund; in the sense that these are sufficiently numerous and repetitive, there is indeed a "flow" of revenue into the area of operations. However, it is inaccurate to speak of revenue as a flow of *funds* unless the cash basis of accounting is implied; even then it is better to refer to the cash proceeds from customer dealings as "collections" to keep clear the meaning of revenue as opposed to cash receipts.[6] Revenue is observed from the addition of new assets—which may be, but do not necessarily have to be, cash.[7] Although there are a number of transactions from which new assets may arise, it is not difficult to distinguish revenue from the rest; the equity notion that has been presented offers a clean-cut basis for making distinctions between revenue and other things. Revenue differs from other asset-increasing transactions in that the new assets are completely free of equity restrictions other than the residual equity of the fund itself.

Financing transactions do not establish revenue; there are always involved certain specific restrictions on the assets acquired. For example, the acquisition of labor service or material goods on credit (as indeed such things nearly always are) is a matter of contract. In the express or implied provisions of the contract certain equities are recognized in terms of contingent money payments or other commitments easily determinable from attendant facts.

The "sale" of a bond issue by a corporation brings new assets into the fund, but it also entails future obligations with respect to the payment of interest and reimbursement of the principal, at least in event of liquidation.[8] The issuance of other securities such as preferred or common shares may seem to be different, but the situation is really quite parallel to the case of bonds. These securities always entail certain restrictions which accounting records as equities; these may involve various kinds of rights with respect to dividends, participation in voting control, privileges of subscription to new stock issues, as well as some kind of contingent financial claim, for example, the legal preference in dividends or assets as to preferred shares or the ultimate claims in liquidation of common stock. These restrictions are entirely sufficient to distinguish investments, as a variety of financing transaction, from any conception of revenue.

Similarly, a customer deposit against the future delivery of goods or services is not revenue, because of the explicit understanding that the failure to complete the arrangement by delivery will necessitate the return of the deposited amount; rentals received in advance are subject to the restriction of future delivery of service and are therefore not revenue until this requirement has been satisfied.

Revaluations are not transactions but belated recognitions of economic effects that have occurred. The principal issue here is whether or not such effects should be recognized, and this is a problem of valuation, not of terminology. However, if valuations at higher or lower figures than have appeared on the books are to be recognized, there are still restrictions to be considered in recording such valuations. The unit of measurement in accounting is a temporal one, in that it has meaning only for a given economic situation—even cash is subject to this qualification:

> A man does not value money for its own sake, but for its purchasing power—that is to say, for what it will buy. Therefore, his demand is not for units of money as such, but for units of general purchasing power. Since, however, there is no means of holding general purchasing power except in the form of money, his demand for purchasing power translates itself into a demand for an "equivalent" quantity of money.[9]

Thus, a change in the valuation of fixed assets is in part a recognition of the change in the meaning of "money." This may, and should, operate as a restriction upon the asset amount added to the fund; it merely adjusts (to conform to the new meaning of "money") those restrictions which were placed against the asset when it was originally acquired. Of course, it is often true that the appraisal involves new (or hitherto unrecognized) services or corrections of past errors. The problem of separating the influences bearing upon a given appraisal is indeed a difficult one, and one may easily agree with Marple that "it is best to think of revaluation surplus as a temporary suspense or adjustment account applying against the net worth section of the balance sheet as a whole."[10] However, the terminological problem of distinguishing appraisal credits from revenue hinges upon (*a*) whether or not additional services have been added to the fund and (*b*) what, if any, restrictions ought to be set up as applying to the new values, however derived or measured.

Viewed from the standpoint of fund theory and the attendant service concepts, the question of whether gifts, donations, bequests, or discoveries give rise to revenue can be approached with the same tools. A completely unrestricted gift or bequest which meets the test for added service potentials in the fund must be regarded as revenue.[11] Although it may be argued that this kind of revenue should be segregated because of its special nature and nonrecurring character, this argument applies to classification and reporting methods, not to the nature of revenue. Unrestricted gifts establish revenue credits in government and institution accounts;[12] there is no reason why the principle should be different in one field of accounting than it is in another. Discoveries, like revaluations, must meet the test of whether there are in fact added service potentials in the fund as a result of the discovery; if there are, the absence of restrictions upon these new service potentials establishes the presence of revenue.

However, the restrictions that do apply to gifts, bequests, or donations—indeed, any restrictions applicable to assets in any fund—must be interpreted in the light of the purpose and the activities of the fund. In the case of an endowment the fact that the donated assets must be invested and the principal maintained indefinitely prevents the recognition of revenue from the gift. But the new assets produced by the investment of the original gift are unrestricted so far as the endowment fund is concerned, and they therefore establish revenue for that fund.

It may be objected, at this point, that the concept of revenue presented here does not permit the direct addition of fund revenues to establish the total revenue for the aggregation of funds of the entire institution. The criteria that have been proposed would permit a given transaction to be considered as revenue in one fund but not in some other one; hence the total revenue of the institution as a whole would depend upon the number and the nature of the funds that happen to be established. The reply to this objection is that this is precisely as it should be, for the revenue of the institution as a whole is not necessarily the sum of its parts. The same situation applies to orthodox theories in the case of corporate entities. If the various departments of a business are considered as but one fund, the meaning of revenue is different from that applicable to separate corporations, partnership or proprietorships. The consideration of the effects of "intercompany" transactions is always taken into account when the statements of corporate businesses are "consolidated," for precisely this reason. Fund theory cannot change the boundaries of situations that are considered in the establishment of funds; if the definition of the fund is changed (by the preparation of "suprafund" statements or by other means), the concepts of assets, equities, revenue, and expense must be applied so as to fit the new and different situation.

A somewhat peculiar situation arises when assets other than those normally considered to be the "product" of the firm are exchanged for other assets. There are two cases here, however, that should be kept distinct. As an instance of the first, suppose a manufacturer to make an exchange of one item of machinery for a similar item—the so-called "exchange in kind." Tax authorities declare this to be a strictly nongain or loss transaction; accounting theorists, however, would be willing to recognize the possibility of gain or loss in such a transaction but would insist that it is not a revenue transaction, on the grounds that the machinery is not the product of the firm and that the transaction is of nonrecurring nature. These arguments are not particularly satisfying, for the difficulty of specifying the product of a firm may in some cases make for trouble in applying the rule; further, such transactions may and do occur frequently in some lines of business. The criteria that have been proposed offer at least reasonable grounds for judging the transaction; (1) if there are new assets actually added to the fund and (2) there are no specific restrictions (apart from those which indicate the nature of the fund) applicable to these new assets, the proceeds of such an exchange are revenue. Applying the first criterion poses a question of the same character as the one raised in connection with revaluations; applying the second test usually shows an absence of restrictions. So far as this test applies, there should seldom be objection to treating such an exchange transaction as a revenue item, even though the revenue be segregated as a special kind. The second case of fixed asset exchanges, in which the asset is sold for cash, would seem even less difficult; the principal problem here is whether or not book values measure the cost of the exchange. The tests of revenue are nearly always met in the cash exchange transaction.

Turning now to that large group of transactions which add assets to the fund in terms of the proceeds of regular product sales, the criteria that have been suggested apply equally well to clarify the concept. A sale, of itself, does not establish revenue conclusively; the question as to whether there are restrictions that should be recognized must be met. A conditional sale does not result in revenue, even though cash is transferred into the fund by such sale; for the condition or restriction in the sale contract makes the deal a financing transaction until the restriction is removed. Sales that involve commitments with respect to service maintenance, guaranties, and return, exchange, or adjustment privileges establish revenue only to the extent that these commitments do not apply. It is conventional practice in such cases to make "allowances" for the probable amounts thus restricted, reducing the billed price by such amount to arrive at a revenue figure. The problem of uncollectible accounts is perhaps similar to these, but this seems to be as much a matter of prudence in valuation as it is of restriction. Discounts offered fall into the same category as uncollectibles; perhaps these do not so much involve restrictions upon the new assets as they enter into the computation of the value to be placed upon them.

The foregoing analysis and exposition avoids entirely the "tests" of revenue frequently advocated by accounting writers, such as "earning," "realization," and "distributability." The confusion that exists as to the meaning of these tests, and the lack of specifications as to the ways in which they are to be applied, tend to reduce their significance for the guidance of accounting practice. It is worth while to review some of what has been written concerning these "tests."

Kester, in a discussion of "unearned income," cites the examples of royalties, rents, magazine subscriptions, and fares collected but tickets not yet taken up as examples of unearned revenue; he points out that payments for such services "are frequently and normally received in advance of the fiscal period when the facilities they represent will be employed by those to whom the business unit offers its goods and services. Deferred income, therefore, is a liability to render service or to furnish goods."[13]

This would suggest that the earning of income is the extinguishment of the equity that restricts the asset fund upon receipt of the advance payment. However, in a later exposition concerned with "realized and unrealized profits" he writes:

> Profits may be said to be realized when the corporation need do nothing further to enjoy the benefit of them. . . . . Thus, if due provision is made, in the way of additional costs, for any further incidental service needed to complete the earning of the income, income is best taken in the period in which sale and delivery are made. . . . . A commercial bank which collects its interest income at time of discounting a depositor's note, does not claim the income as realized at time of collection, because it has not rendered the service entitling it to the income. Day by day as it allows the use of its funds by the borrower, the interest income is being earned; it is becoming realized.[14]

From another source there appears to be a further explanation for the treatment of advance payments of this character:

> Fundamentally, the accounting postulate that income is earned at the time of sale is based upon the conception of the passing of legal title. Since in the majority of cases in which deposits are received in advance goods are not definitely segregated as the property of the prospective buyer, however, they cannot be considered as sold. In many cases, the goods or services ordered are not even produced at the time the deposit is received. Cash deposits should therefore be considered merely as a guarantee of a buyer's good intention.[15]

Paton, in the attempt to distinguish between earned and realized revenue, presents the following discussion:

> There are two main conceptions of "earned" revenue. Many would agree with the proposition that revenue is earned in a fundamental sense with the process of operation or, more precisely, with the accumulation of costs assignable to product. The principal alternative view considers revenue to be effectively earned only when the final product is delivered or furnished. A special application of the second conception is found in the interpretation of accrued interest, rent, etc., as earned. Increase in value in the form of accretion or appreciation is in a sense "earned" in the period or periods in which the enhancement occurs.
>
> Earning should not be identified with realization. Revenue is fully "realized," according to the usual position, when it is represented by or supported by cash receipts, and it has become conventional to treat bona-fide current

receivables as the equivalent of cash in this connection. Similarly the values represented by accretion or appreciation are viewed as unrealized until they are converted to cash or receivables, although a case can be made for the position that some forms of accretion (natural increase in a marketable herd, for example) are substantially realized.

. . . . Under the thoroughgoing production basis of revenue accounting, as outlined earlier, revenue is booked which although earned has not been realized. (In the case of a job taken on a cost-plus contract, revenue earned on the basis of percentage of completion may perhaps be viewed as realized.) Under the sale and collection bases the revenue recognized has been both earned and realized.[16]

The real issues that are outlined in the discussion of earning versus realization seem to be closely parallel to the criteria we have suggested: (*a*) whether or not there are new assets (realization) and (*b*) whether or not the restrictions in the sale contract have been satisfied (earning). However, it is interesting to see just what may be involved in the notion of realization, as conceived of in terms of cash or claims to cash.

The weakness of a strict cash basis of accounting, especially on the cost side, was made clear by Paton:

As was stated above, the view that collection is the proper signal for income entries is consistent with the theory that payment is the accounting evidence of purchase. Evidently if this theory were actually adopted with respect to the recognition of cost incurred it would mean in extreme cases that materials would be acquired, manufactured and sold for cash prior to their acquisition from an accounting standpoint. In other words, the appearance of cash revenue might antedate the recognition of some of the actual costs of this revenue, an obviously ridiculous state of affairs.[17]

This statement shows clearly the weakness in the cash basis of accounting. But the cash receipts test for realization of revenue is weak for precisely the same reasons which cover cash disbursements as a test of cost. Although it may be "conservative" to employ the cash basis for revenue and the accrual basis for costs, such a procedure cannot be adopted in any realistic approach to accounting; practice has therefore rejected the strict cash collection test for realization of revenue.

The "claims to cash" criterion developed by Gilman suggests that realization of revenue is established by the creation of cash claims: "The test of realization, therefore, demands an actual immediate or deferred effect upon cash, the time lag involved in any deferment being no element of the test."[18]

This at first seems to be a useful criterion, until the full implications are brought out in further discussion:

It is the cash aspect of the exchange that represents the primary test of realization, whereas the time elapsing between the receipt of a good claim to cash and the actual receipt of the cash itself really has no significance, although admittedly important from the practical financial viewpoint. . . . . In any specific instance the test for realization is found in the question: will the relinquishment of merchandise result in cash or in the creation of an asset which, in the normal course of events, will be converted into cash, i.e., *does any further selling have to take place in order to obtain cash?*[19]

This "absence of additional sale" is employed in Gilman's discussion to the exclusion of other factors; he disregards explicitly the current status of the asset received in exchange and the fair market value of the asset, dismissing these as "expedients having no place in the development of a theory of accounting profit."[20] The illustration he employs as an "exaggeration test" brings this out clearly:

A used car dealer, for example, has on hand two identical Ford cars each carrying a price tag of $250. He sells one to a customer, and receives in exchange therefor a ten year interest bearing note for $250. The other car is sold to a customer in exchange for five shares of General Motors stock which has an instant and ready market. . . . . Disregarding the intentionally exaggerated and unnatural character of these transactions, the sale of the first car for a ten year note clearly results in realized income. In spite of the unusual time lag a note represents a claim to cash. The exchange of the automobile for five shares of General Motors stock, on the other hand, cannot result in true realized income, nor as a matter of theoretical accuracy is income ever realized on this particular kind of a transaction.

Capital stock of General Motors or of any other company is not a legal claim to cash. When and if the General Motors stock is sold, realized income may result but it should be noted that this income is from the sale of the stock and not from the sale of the automobile. In the hands of the automobile dealer this General Motors stock is an asset which merely replaces the used car and which takes the same value.[21]

This illustration is not conclusive; if it be changed so that the dealer might have sold a car on either basis, it is not difficult to see which he would prefer. However sound may be the present position of the purchaser whose note is offered in exchange, the service significance of the note is far less than that of the easily effected conversion of General Motors stock to cash. It is to be noted that *both* alternatives involve the acceptance of a chose in action that involves some risk; but the risk is readily and finally terminable in the one case, and it cannot be gotten rid of except by shifting at a cost in the other. For, if the note is held to maturity, the events of the future have a weighty bearing upon the nature of this "claim to cash"; the fortunes of both buyer and seller are bound together in the document, and this cannot be escaped by discounting the note. The only way in which the note can be viewed apart from the credit of the maker is by selling it—transferring the claim to some other person without warranty and without recourse. Thus the sale is just as necessary in the case of the note as it is in the case of the General Motors stock. To contrast the sale of an unsecured, single-name paper in an unorganized market with the transfer of a listed stock of a well-known corporation through organized exchange channels is to arrive at the reverse of Gilman's conclusion. The fallacy in his argument is that the note is not a "claim to cash" at all but a claim against a *person*, who may or may not control an asset fund of sufficient size or liquidity to pay the note now or when it matures.

Gilman's argument does not stop here, however; he goes on to point out that an exchange for bonds or a mortgage would be accepted as a basis for realization, although an exchange for office equipment or tools used by the seller in his business would not. This attitude places an inordinate confidence in "cash claims" to measure service potentiality. There are many instances in which cash is actually an undesirable asset; whenever prices are rising, and seem certain to rise further, cash balances beyond the day-to-day requirements for carrying on business are actually risky from a sound economic point of view. Cash earns no return unless invested, and it has no significance except for what it will buy. The realities of economic life are not bound up in cash accounts, however much wishful thinking the accountant may want to do about it!

There is still more to this argument that needs discussion. Assuming that the car cost the dealer $200, Gilman goes on to point out that actual cash transactions are not always required to support income realization, for he says:

An immediate or subsequent cash account entry is not necessarily the result of a sales transaction upon which income is truly realized. Income may be realized under such assumed conditions as the following, which uses the same illustration as before. The automobile dealer may owe his customer $300 and may offer to settle that indebtedness by turning over to him the Ford car. The question then arises as to whether income has been realized by the transaction, since the cash account is not affected. As a matter of fact, the cash position is affected as the $300 debt is a bona-fide liability, since the dealer's cash account, if this arrangement was split into its elements, would eventually be $300 smaller because of the required payment of the liability, and would be $250 greater because of the sale of the car, this diminution and addition representing the normal expectancy resulting from the fruition of claim and counter-claim were they not offset against each other.

In this illustration the dealer enjoys two different kinds of gains; one of $50 upon sale of the car, and one of $50 from liquidation of the liability at a discount.[22]

This analysis is really inconsistent with what has already been said by Gilman. Is it not just as reasonable to postulate similar cash transactions in the case of the General Motors stock? Such procedure would certainly be more justifiable when the transactions are supportable by market prices that are quoted publicly!

A view that is a bit more liberal than the "cash or claims to cash" position with respect to realization is presented by one writer in the following terms:

> Profits are realized by sales or exchanges in which the value received is greater than the cost (or book value) of the thing parted with. It is not necessary that the profit be realized in cash; profits are regarded as realized if cash or property is received in the transaction, or if the transaction creates a valid claim against a solvent debtor.[23]

This statement agrees in substance with the criterion of addition of new service units to the fund (presumably, it would also call for the absence of restrictions upon those new service units), but it suggests that revenue is somehow bound up with a sale transaction. This permits of two possible interpretations: (*a*) that a sale is merely a prerequisite to revenue recognition, that is, the sale must precede the recognition of revenue, or (*b*) that the sale is coincident with the revenue entry—that it serves as the signal for bringing the revenue upon the record. These will be discussed separately.

The thesis that sale is prerequisite to revenue is not borne out by practice, especially in some areas of accounting. Investment income is a case in point. The recognition of investment income, in the form of interest or dividends receivable, does have foundation in the legal and economic environment in which they are recorded, but there is no sale transaction connected with such recognition. The contractual basis in the form of a financing transaction is not a sale; there is no final and conclusive transfer of service that characterizes a sale as apart from a financing deal.

The application of accounting to the operations of government and eleemosynary funds is hampered by such a concept of revenue. Governments and eleemosynary institutions deliver service far and wide; some of these services are paid for explicitly in the form of fees and licenses, tuition, dues, and the like. But most of the activities of funds such as these do not reduce to a sale basis, for the reason not only that the recipients of services from such funds do not engage in any contractual relations that could be interpreted as sales but that these recipients are but seldom the same persons who are asked to contribute to the maintenance of the fund. If the contract of sale is absent from these operations, must it be true that there can be no revenue for investment, government, and eleemosynary funds? The sale contract is not a prerequisite to the recognition of revenue; if the sale does have relevance to the revenue notion, it must be through the medium of timing.

The notion that the sale is the signal for making revenue entries is one that has gained wide acceptance. Paton says:

> In the first place, revenue arises primarily as a result of business activity and must be recognized and measured in terms of the essential features of operation. Second, revenue must be evidenced and supported by genuine asset values, preferably in liquid form. In enterprises producing or dealing in commodities the fundamental requirements are met, it is usually agreed, by accepting the completed sale as the test of revenue. The sale is viewed as the most significant of the chain of events making up the business process, the end toward which all efforts are directed. Upon the occasion of sale the product is separated from the producing business by delivery to the customer, or is earmarked for future delivery. The sale, moreover, brings into being new assets in the form of cash or receivables.[24]

But, even here, it must be observed, the sale transaction must sometimes be disregarded as a signal for revenue recognition. The mere contract of sale does not establish the presence of revenue; this is not only because there are a number of areas in which sale contracts do not exist (as has been pointed out above) but also because the contract of sale is often so *unimportant* in the sequence of operations as to be almost undiscernible. Water sold by a public utility company on the basis of a monthly or quarterly "rental" (average charge) basis through the company's mains; professional services of an advertising, legal, or consulting engineer firm; the construction of buildings, bridges, or other similar projects; continuing maintenance or repair and adjustment contracts—all are instances in which the sale is but an incident in the real flow of activities.

The signal for the recognition of revenue in these cases is really the rendering of the service, or the delivery of the goods—the release of "expense," not the sale contract itself. In theory every sale contract involves both rights and duties, and it is the execution of the contract by the seller that really constitutes the basis for recognizing revenue. The fact that the new assets arise from the operation of legal or equitable rules does not mean that assets are legal claims; rather, the legal claims are evidence of assets, and it is the assets themselves that support the revenue credit. The concept of "matching revenue with costs" is meaningless unless there be some act common to both revenue recognition and cost release that can be identified; this is the rendering of service, not the "making of a sale." The sale criterion for timing thus gives way to the rendering of service; this is, at least in theory, equivalent to the removal of restrictions against assets. The sale could be recorded as a contingent asset—one coupled with a specific equity; the delivery or "earmarking" of goods, or the delivery of the service required by the contract has the effect of giving the contingent asset real significance, by satisfying the equity that was established at the outset. Thus are justified the two criteria that were proposed for the recognition of revenue: the existence of new service units and the absence of restrictions against them.

INCOME

The typical conception of income is that of the net resultant of the flows of revenue and expense; it might, therefore, seem that income would raise but few and minor issues, once the components of income had been described. This, however, is not the case; there are certain basic issues that are raised with respect to income which have important implications for fund theory.

It is indeed unfortunate that "income" has a personal connotation; that is, that income is generally conceived of as accruing to the benefit of some *person*. Much of the difference between the proprietary and the entity views of accounting stems from the personal implications of "income." To the proprietary theorist income is the increase in the proprietor's net worth which arises from the operations of his business (as opposed to investments or disinvestments of his capital). In other words, income from the proprietary standpoint is the gain *to the proprietor* that is created by the transactions which have occurred.

However, the stockholders of a corporation are not "owners" in the same sense that proprietors and partners are. Even when his investment and withdrawal of capital are coincident to the formation and dissolution of the corporate organization, the stockholder is not a manager, except in a very restricted sense; the divorcement of management from the ownership attributes of proprietorship means that the stockholder is but a limited and special variety of "owner." The stockholder differs from the traditional "proprietor" in terms of risk factors also; this arises not only from the limited liability feature of corporate finance but also from the fact that the stockholder may diversify his holdings, leaving his "investment" scattered over a number of widely different areas, so as to minimize the risk attached to his investment as a whole. These factors, together with the fact that different types of stock are available in even one given company, mean that the risk aspect of ownership is different in the case of a stockholder from what it is in the case of a partner or proprietor. It is not surprising, in view of these elements in the situation, that the stockholder does not take the same kind of interest in the corporate affairs as might be expected of an "owner"; it necessarily follows that, to a stockholder, income from corporate operations is quite a different thing from partnership or venture income. The notion of income which seems so clear and direct in the simple forms of business organization is hopelessly confused and confounded when applied to the corporate situation. There is no person to whom the income concept can be related, unless it be the fictitious legal creation, or an assumed "entity."

Thus, the "entity" conception of income is born out of necessity; the revenue and expense of the corporation's operations are related to a purely hypothetical person, so as to provide a "recipient" for income. This, of course, simplifies the immediate situation, and it also simplifies the reporting procedures; the financial reports are the reports of "entity" operations and are concerned with the things that appear to be of importance to the "entity." However, this is merely a cutting of the Gordian knot—the immediate difficulty is resolved but at the expense of relevance in the result. "Entity income" is not a meaningful concept, for the income figure as calculated has relevance only to a personality that does not exist. This is an anomalous situation. Of what significance is "income" related to a purely conjectural and imaginary person?

In order to have significance for the investor or stockholder, entity income must be related to the factors that are significant in the present or prospective stockholder-investor's situation. Therefore, the investor must interpret the entity income figure by analyzing its components and by making such adjustments and recalculations as are needed to fit his case. His "investment" does not coincide with book values anywhere in the balance sheet, and the valuations of certain kinds of assets may be quite different for his purposes than they would be for partnership or proprietorship situations. To illustrate, fixed assets are for the investor merely sunk costs; these are significant to him only because these facilities must be maintained and/or replaced (in kind or in service) if the normal expense stream is to be continued in the future. Amortizations of cost (or other valuations) of such facilities are significant to the investor only to the extent that they *may* measure the provision for such maintenance or replacement that ought to be considered in the light of current developments. Inventories, from the investor's position, are the sources of gains and losses through speculation when prices change; the amounts and kinds of inventory on hand are important to the investor to the extent that there are inherent advantages from the current market viewpoint in the holding of them. The timing of speculative gains on the criterion of "realization" is simply wrong so far as the investor is concerned. The separation of speculative gains from transaction margins is highly important from the investor's viewpoint, however difficult it may be to separate them, or however inconsequential this may seem from the entity standpoint. The entity income figure is not only of itself quite irrelevant to the investor's problem, but the data that are conventionally presented to support this calculation are frequently useless for his purposes. The really important data for investors' decisions are often either buried in the massing of figures in the income statement, or they are reflected only in balance-sheet changes that are at best not too easily interpreted. The fund statement helps to relieve this situation somewhat, but the content and the function of this statement are still none too clear to either the readers or those who prepare it, as we shall see in a later connection. Entity income is neither synonymous with investor income, nor can entity calculations be readily translated into meaningful data for the investor, so far as the orthodox form of income report is concerned.

From the point of view of another "interest"—that of management—the usefulness of an entity income concept is also questionable. Management, regardless of the form or the nature of the business operations, is concerned with the making of choices between alternative courses of action. It is true that the effects of managerial decisions are at some time and in some way shown in the entity income figure; but the fact remains that these effects are distributed through time and are never completely traceable one by one into the final result. Many a wise and desirable managerial decision is not reflected in the income statement until years after the decision was made. Often, the effects of various decisions are so mingled in a given income statement that the only result is an average of unknown weighting and of therefore dubious significance. Often the effects of noncontrollable factors—such as technological progress, shifts in the market, the actions of competitors—are such as to cover up entirely the effects of managerial activities upon income. Management decisions are based upon narrowly defined and strictly prescribed kinds of data; and managerial accounting is something quite different from the preparation and interpretation of entity statements. Rather, the accounting system must provide for management purposes the kinds of detailed information upon which choices are to be based; these data are seldom portrayed in conventional financial statements for the enterprise as a whole. Classification, statistical analysis, extrapolations, and interpretations of operating data are needed for managerial control. Over-all totals and averages from conventional income statements and balance sheets are only rarely significant for managerial purposes.

Management is concerned fully as much with what ought to be, or with what might have been, as it is with the actual events that occur. Any real desire to profit by mistakes or to learn from experience must entail a comparison of actual events with expectations. From the management viewpoint, savings and wastes are the real sources of profit or loss. But data on savings and wastes certainly do not appear in entity income statements, if indeed the entity view would regard them as relevant at all. The management view of accounting is not at all akin to the "entity" view; first, because the kinds of data that seem significant from the entity viewpoint are not usable in making managerial decisions unless carefully reinterpreted and analyzed in terms of the specific managerial problems that are involved and, second, because the entity view excludes or buries precisely the kinds of information that may be most important to the managerial problem. Although there may be validity in the statement that entity income does in the final analysis represent a test of over-all management, this test is far too crude and much too vague and general to serve either as an appraisal of over-all managerial efficiency or as a guide for managerial decision.

From the standpoint of various social control agencies that may have an interest in accounting data, it is obvious that the income notion is not at all a clear concept.[25] A mere acquaintance with the general framework of rules and regulations for computing income for tax purposes is sufficient to establish that the income concept that is employed in taxation is neither the same as the entity notion of income nor, in the last analysis, more than a rigidly defined method of calculation designed to simplify(?) administration of the tax laws. Other social control agencies tend to establish their own rules, to the extent of prescribing uniform systems of accounting, as well as standard forms of reports; only in rare instances do the concepts thus established coincide with any definitely defined notions of income.

The implications of what has been said above concerning the income concept may seem far-reaching, especially since the accountant traditionally has maintained that the prime function of accounting is to measure and report income. The difficult nature of a multimeaningful concept of income would seem to limit, if it does not obliterate, this function of accounting. However, the measurement of income is not the sole, or even the most important, aim of accounting; in fact, there are grounds for the belief that the accountant has overemphasized and overworked the notion of income far past the point of diminishing returns. The question of what is to be included and excluded from income and the measurement aspects of certain situations with respect to income have taken precedence over other aspects of financial reporting that are not only easier to deal with but also more important!

It is impossible to present a single income figure that will begin to meet all the demands which will be made upon it; further, the overemphasis upon income calculation puts undesirable limits on not only the form but the significance of financial reports. The pre-eminence of an income figure in a financial report not only implies that that figure has a specific significance to all readers but suggests finality and precision of measurement which cannot be achieved, even if the conceptual difficulties are waved aside. It may well be that accountants should avoid the complications, confusions, and disappointments which arise from overemphasis upon "net income."

There is some evidence of accountants' awareness of the limitations of income reporting. Discussions of the problems associated with the accounting period[26] are part of this. Although it is true that periodic reporting must "sever many living threads" and that "there can be no wholly dependable computation of net income until the particular enterprise has run its course," it must also be remembered that income is itself a time-period concept. And, although the computation of periodic income may be a highly technical (and not generally useful) diagnosis, the calculation of income at the conclusion of an enterprise is but financial autopsy! Income—even in the technical and conventional sense in which the term is employed by accountants—is not a precisely determinable quantity of broad objective significance. This is recognized in the wording of professional audit certificates; and current trends in the form and arrangement of financial reports bear this out.

The "combined statement of income and surplus" advocated originally by the American Accounting Association[27] and later given some measure of recognition by the American Institute of Accountants[28] is worth considering in this connection. The underlying thought which motivates this presentation was put by one writer in the following terms: "No one figure should be accorded undue importance as earnings per share, but that the entire story is essential to a full understanding."[29] The purpose of the combined statement was certainly not only to assure the publication of the details of surplus adjustments, for this aim could as well be achieved by the emphatic requirement of a statement of surplus to accompany the income statement; what was really intended is fairly clear—to call attention to the tentative nature of the net annual income figure.

There have been attempts to work toward this objective—reduced emphasis upon the single-year income figure—by the use of comparative and averaged statements. Paton says: "As some of us have been recommending for a long time, accountants should make more use of comparative, cumulative, and average income statements, as a means of throwing the single period statement in proper perspective."[30] Although there are other reasons for them, the provisions of the income-tax laws that provide for "carry-overs" and "carry-backs" are at least to some extent a recognition that the annual income figure is not a final and conclusive one.

It may seem to the reader that the present argument is directed at abolition of the statement of operations, but such is not the case. The operating report should show all the detail that is now considered good practice and more; the point to be made is that there is no reason why the statement has to be arranged in such a way as to emphasize or even calculate an annual net income figure. Rather, the data that are important to the readers of accounting statements should be presented in such a way as to allow the computation of an income figure that meets the need or the desires of the reader. It might be said that it would be desirable to force the reader of the statement to make his own calculations of income from the data thus presented. There is a most effective way to do these things, if we can accept the notion that the aim of operating statements is broader than the mere production of a single amount to represent the income for the year.

One other phase of the income problem needs to be examined here; this involves a "test" of income that is sometimes considered in discussions of revenue—the test of distributability. Although this criterion has not received as much attention from writers on accounting as have the others which have been mentioned, it has some importance because of its implications for sound theory. The nature of the distributability test is quite clearly put by Cotter in the following terms: "The ability of one company to pay out all the profit it shows without impairment of original assets, and the inability of the other to do the same thing, indicates quite clearly which had real and which had 'fool's profits.' "[31]

The opposing point of view is presented by Paton in these words:

> The term "paper profits" is often applied to the increase in market value of assets such as securities and occasionally is used in referring to earnings which have been realized through sale and immediately reinvested. . . . . Are profits that are fully realized and recognizable in terms of individual transactions rendered invalid as an expression of periodic income because the funds represented have been absorbed in inventories or other forms of assets not immediately available for dividends? In other words, is income not to be reported because the necessities of business operation have required the retention of the corresponding funds in the business? Unless the established procedures and conceptions associated with the measurement of business income are to be radically changed, a negative answer to such questions is justified. Earned and realized income is not necessarily distributable income; a distinction should be drawn between income performance and income administration.[32]

Applying the test of distributability to revenue is logically impossible, for it is not revenue but *assets* that are distributed. And, under legal notions of what constitutes proper dividend action, the amounts distributed must be unrestricted, that is, assets in excess of equity restrictions for liabilities, invested capital, and (as the statutes may happen to recognize them) certain kinds of surplus. Again, the distributability test cannot be applied to *revenue*, for there must also be taken into account the fact that coincident with the revenue flow is the corresponding expense stream. Therefore, if distributability is a test of any phase of operating data, it must apply to income, because the revenue effect alone is incomplete as a creator of assets—expense usually is prerequisite to revenue. Only the net effect of the revenue and expense streams can be considered in approaching the problem of distributing those assets to stockholders. Thus, to apply distributability as a test of income recognition involves examination of the assets and equities which have arisen from the revenue and expense flows. At the very least distributability implies that income must be related to specific assets to which the test can be applied. Also, there must be some rules as to what assets can be considered as distributable. These cannot require that distribution be limited to cash, for that would entail a cash theory of income—the evils of which need no elaboration here. In addition, since there must be some amount of various kinds of assets—including cash—kept within the fund so that regular operations can be carried on, there would ensue the need for standards of the amount and kinds of working or other assets that the firm would have to retain within the fund. Such standards would be impossible to establish except upon the most arbitrary bases, since financial administration can vary not only as between different kinds of industry but also as between enterprises engaged in substantially the same activities. The distributability test for income recognition is obviously an unfeasible one; accounting has enough problems of its own without the attempt to apply standards of financial administration to the reporting of financial events.

The income concept as a whole is a tenuous notion. It is at least partly a matter of point of view as to what is meant by the term in the first place, because of its personal implications. Certainly the entity notion of income is no solution to this problem, and the proprietary view involves too many complications for its use in modern forms of business organization. There is good reason to argue that the accountant should confine himself to the reporting of business events, without attempting to report in a single figure (or a set of calculations directed at that single figure) the final *result* of operations. There is even some evidence that accountants would welcome a release from the problems and the difficulties that stem from overemphasizing income measurement as the goal of accounting. As has been suggested, and as will appear in detail in a later discussion, it is possible to avoid entirely the confusions associated with the notion of income by focusing attention upon the *fund* rather than the persons that are interested in it.

SUMMARY

Neither the proprietary nor the entity theory of accounting has been able to solve the basic problems of accounting theory. This is in part due to the fact that almost invariably the discussion of an issue has been clouded by the valuation aspects of the situation; but it is even more attributable to the fact that both the proprietary and the entity view start from a *person* to whom, or for whom, or about whom, the accounting reports are made. We have specifically removed the question of valuation from discussion here and have presented the basic interest of accounting in impersonal terms as the *fund*. The recognition that assets are service potentials provides both operational content and homogeneity of substance for accounting terminology. Thus the concept of assets is related clearly to the expense stream and the corresponding flow of revenue. Equities are not claims or obligations, nor are they mere legal liabilities; rather, they represent the restrictions that apply to the fund of assets. The equality of assets and equities rests on the fact of residual equity, not on the idea that property "belongs" to someone or that some fictitious person must account to owners for the assets intrusted to it.

We have established the test of expense and revenue in the asset notion and the effects of equity restrictions and have rejected the concepts of realization, earning, distributability, and the like; these are but terms that describe what is done rather than basic reasons for doing it. Similarly, we have rejected the notion of income because of the difficulties that arise from the personal associations and interpretations that are embodied in such a concept as can be evolved in operational terms.

Thus, we now have a few basic ideas with which to attack the problem of accounting theory: the notion of a fund, a service concept of assets, a restriction concept of equities, and a recognition that expense and revenue are basic *flows*, not specific effects of individual transactions. What can be done with these ideas will occupy the remaining pages of this discussion.

CHAPTER IV

ILLUSTRATIONS AND APPLICATIONS OF FUND THEORY

THE preceding pages have served to present a system of ideas, or a set of basic premises, for the development of the fund theory of accounting. However much this approach may differ from the "entity" or "proprietary" views in its fundamental aspects, the fund theory does not in fact involve any far-flung changes in extant procedures or systems of accounting. Actually, fund theory establishes a broader and more logical basis for what is already considered good practice in accounting; in addition, there are some aspects of accounting that may be improved by application of the fund theory, both in terms of the areas in which fund theory is already expressed in practice and in terms of the kinds of improvements that may be developed by application of fund theory to specific situations.

INSTITUTION AND GOVERNMENT ACCOUNTS

Fund theory is most clearly exhibited in those accounting procedures that are applied to institution and government situations. Here it is that funds are recognized explicitly in the accounting statements as well as in financial reports. As a backdrop for the exposition attempted in this chapter, it seems desirable to review briefly the elements of the fund accounting process as it relates to institution and government operations.

A fund, as defined by the National Committee on Standard Reports for Institutions of Higher Education, is "a sum of money or other resources set aside for the purpose of carrying on specific activities or attaining certain objects in accordance with special regulations, restrictions, or limitations."[1]

In this statement a fund appears as a unit of activity represented by a collection of assets; since the operations of the fund entail the acquisition and disposition of assets of various kinds, the fund accounts will also include those accounts that record the restrictions or limitations which apply to the use of the assets—"equities" as they have been described in a previous part of this discussion. Some assets will be received free of any restrictions other than those implied in the definition of the fund; thus arises the notion of revenue to be reflected in special accounts. Since the operations also involve the release of services to attain the objectives for which the fund is established, expense accounts will also appear in the financial records of the fund.

However clearly the institution as a whole may be recognized as a legal entity, the legal entity is not the basis for fund accounting. The purposes to be served by the various operations within the institution may differ from each other to a considerable extent; some assets and their corresponding equities, expenses, and revenues may be of such special nature as to warrant separate classification and accounting; in any event, the managerial and operating responsibilities are specifically detailed. Funds established for these reasons maintain in the accounting structure the distinctions that are important in financial administration. The emphasis in establishing funds is upon the definition of areas of operation, not upon legal or other forms of personality.

The view of a fund as an accounting unit is recognized even more explicitly in the government field. The National Committee on Municipal Accounting defines a fund as "a sum of money or other resources (gross or net) set aside for the purpose of carrying on specific activities or attaining certain objectives in accordance with special regulations, restrictions, or limitations, and constituting an independent fiscal and accounting entity."[2]

Here again the notion of entity is not that of a person, legal or otherwise; the accounting unit is clearly distinguished from any personal implications. This is partly a matter of circumstance, for a fund in government accounting cannot be identified with or related to a specific personality—there is no person for whom the fund accounts are kept or to whom the reports relate. Although there are persons who are closely associated with the fund operations, these are clearly viewed in their managerial or administrative capacities rather than in any sense of personal entity. This is apparent in the fact that there can be "funds within funds"; the National Committee points out that customer deposits in connection with public utilities constitute a "trust fund" which for convenience is carried within the Utility Fund.[3] Also, some of the funds that are recognized in government accounts deal with a segregation of assets not on the basis of personal control and management but because of other specific features. Plant accounts, for instance, are usually carried in a special "fund,"[4] the proceeds of a general bond issue are viewed as revenues of the Bond Fund, although these proceeds are not revenue to the municipality; the liability on a general bond issue that matures in a future year does not appear as an equity in either the General Fund or the Bond Fund, unless it is to be paid off from the resources of these funds.[5]

It is interesting to observe that the notion of entity as applied to the fund unit in government accounting does not of itself involve commitments to any particular basis of valuation. Indeed, terms such as "cost," "value," "income," and the specific issues of valuation that such terms may involve are peculiarly absent from discussions of institution and government accounting.[6]

The "valuation principle," as enunciated by the National Committee on Municipal Accounting, is:

> Inventories of both consumable and permanent property should be kept in subsidiary records controlled by accounts in the general accounting system. The fixed asset accounts should be maintained on the basis of original cost, or the estimated cost if the original cost is not available; or, in the case of gifts, the appraised value at the time received. The computation of depreciation on general municipal fixed assets is not recommended except for unit cost purposes, unless cash for replacement purposes can legally be set aside.[7]

The absence of any reference to entity prerogatives in this statement is in sharp contrast to the position taken by some entity theorists;[8] in any event, this statement of valuation principle is a clear indication of the separability of valuation from other aspects of accounting theory.

The term "equities" does not have much acceptance in government accounting; indeed, the items that are listed on the right side of government balance sheets are usually labeled "obligations" or "liabilities and surplus." But these items are not confined to legal liabilities or equitable claims. One of the principles laid down by the National Committee on Municipal Accounting indicates that commitments represent important restrictions upon fund assets:

> The general accounting system should include budgetary control accounts for both revenues and expenditures.
>
> As soon as purchase orders or contracts are signed, the resulting obligations should be entered at once as encumbrances of the funds and appropriations affected.[9]

This is a sharp departure from commercial and industrial accounting practices. Outstanding purchase orders or contractual commitments are seldom if ever given explicit recognition in the accounts of trading or manufacturing firms, and the "obligations" thus created appear only as footnotes to financial statements. Even then, the principal reason for mentioning such items at all seems to be that of calling attention to possible losses.

The treatment of encumbrances and appropriations[10] in fund accounting suggests that "equities"—or whatever the items on the right-hand side of the balance sheet may be called—are not mere legal liabilities. Rather, these items seem to be viewed clearly as restrictions against the fund of assets, and they serve to earmark portions of the aggregate assets in the fund for specific purposes or to state just what specific provisions must be borne in mind in the management of the assets of the fund. It is true that commercial and industrial accounting follow this same line of reasoning in respect to "surplus reserves"; however, this approach is worthy of broader application.

Another idea that seems to be firmly established in the field of fund accounting is that long-term items should be segregated from short-term items not only in the financial reports and balance sheets but in the accounting system. This is also stated by the Committee on Municipal Accounting as a principle, in the following terms:

> A clear segregation should be made between the accounts relating to current assets, liabilities and operations, and those relating to fixed assets and liabilities. With the exception of Working Capital, Utility, or Trust funds, fixed assets should not be carried in the same fund with the current assets but should be set up in a separate self-balancing group of accounts. Similarly, except in Special Assessment and Utility funds, long term liabilities should not be carried with the current liabilities of any fund, but should be shown in a separate self-balancing group of accounts.[11]

It is open to some question as to whether the exceptions noted in the statement just quoted are really to be considered as such; even though the accounts for fixed assets and long-term liabilities are kept in the same ledgers as the short-term and current items for these funds, the balance sheets of Working Capital, Utility, Trust, and Special Assessment funds would still segregate the fixed assets and the long-term debt.[12] This would seem to be a situation best described as a "fund within a fund" rather than as an exception to the general rule. So far as balance sheets are concerned, the separation of fixed from current items is of long standing even in commercial and industrial practice; this principle is observed almost universally, despite the difficulties that may arise in distinguishing between current and long-term items.[13]

With respect to operating statements and income sheets, however, there are marked differences between fund accounting and commercial-industrial practice. Expenditures for fixed assets are treated in commercial-industrial accounting as having no direct relation to expense or to the operating statement; their only relation to the measurement of income as reported on operating statements is through depreciation or amortization of some kind. Government accounting views such expenditures as "expense" of the fund from which the expenditure is made and for the period in which the obligation or commitment occurred. Of course, the acquisition is recorded in the property accounts; to this extent the new asset is regarded as property to be accounted for. But, except in those funds in which unit costs are of importance, depreciation of fixed plant is not computed or recognized as expense. Thus, except for Working Capital and the Utility funds, government accounting practice is to record fixed asset acquisitions as expense and to ignore depreciation upon such assets. This may have some justification on the ground that income determination is unimportant in the operations of institutions and governmental agencies; but the case is weak, as has already been pointed out. Whether or not the practice is justifiable, the peculiar treatment of long-term costs in government and institution accounting means that the expense concept is somewhat different in these fields from the one adopted in commercial and industrial accounting.[14]

Aside from the questions of depreciation and amortization, the notion of expense as it is applied in fund accounting differs from the conventional one only in so far as accrual accounting is not followed in the fund accounting scheme and as valuation is a factor in expense measurement.

From the standpoint of revenue, there is not much difference between fund accounting and commercial-industrial concepts. Again, looking to the governmental field, we find that revenues "are defined as 'additions to assets which do not increase any liability nor represent the recovery of an expenditure, and the cancellation of liabilities without a corresponding increase in other liabilities or a decrease in assets.' "[15]

This concept does not differ in essential respects for the conventional notion of revenue; the principal exception is that gifts are, in terms of this definition, acceptable revenue items; whereas conventional accountants view gifts as special transactions, if indeed they are considered at all. Of course, in view of the lack of consideration given to problems of valuation in fund accounting, accretion and revaluation do not fall under the classification of revenues; but the orthodox view is not very different from this, as has been pointed out.

Thus, in summary, the essential differences between fund accounting (as practiced in nonprofit and government situations) and conventional accounting for commercial and industrial activities are:

1. The fund, not some person connected with it, is viewed as an entity.
2. Valuation, so far as fund accounting is concerned, is a minor issue; the absence of income emphasis is largely responsible for this, but the impersonalness of the entity notion obviously contributes to this point of view.
3. Equities, or whatever the right-hand balance sheet items are called, are viewed as restrictions upon assets, not as legal liabilities; this is true not only as to surplus but also with respect to appropriations and commitments.
4. The segregation of long-term from short-term items is maintained in somewhat more definite ways when fund accounting is employed. The funding of capital assets, long-term investments, and the like is common practice in institutional practice.
5. Fund accounting for institutions and government agencies embraces certain procedures in reporting operating data, and there are some differences between financial and institutional concepts of revenue and expense. These differences, however, are largely

matters of valuation or of the degree to which the accrual basis of accounting is followed.

6. One of the distinctive features of fund accounting is the absence of emphasis upon "net income" and related notions of "profit," "operating margins," and the like.

INDUSTRIAL AND FINANCIAL ACCOUNTS—DECENTRALIZED RECORDS

The notion of a fund—in the sense of a specific area of operations which involves certain assets, equities, and corresponding revenue and expense items—is not at all foreign to extant commercial and financial accounting. Although the bookkeeping procedures incident to fund operations may not be evident, and the terminology of fund accounts may not actually appear, it is nevertheless true that many situations are dealt with in ways that involve fund concepts as underlying bases for accounting procedure. One of the fairly obvious cases is the "split-ledger" device which is encountered in factory ledger procedure, branch accounts, and the now not so common "private ledger." Complementary ledgers of the type employed in these situations are justified in practice by the exigencies which arise from decentralization of performance with regard to accounting activities; but they can be justified in theory only by some variant of the fund concept. As in the case of the unincorporated enterprise, the existence of separate accounting records cannot be justified from the viewpoint of legal personality; branches, factories, and the private ledger do not arise from separation of personal entities, and they have none of the attributes of legal or fictitious persons, except as parts of a larger whole. For instance, the unincorporated branch may be separated from the rest of the operations on the ground of location, function, or commodity specialization, or it may be desirable to recognize its unitary significance from the point of view of the delegation of responsibility and authority; but the branch is not a separate entity in any personal or legal sense. The justification for "splitting" the general ledger into complementary parts for the purpose of separating the detailed accounting of the branch from other parts of the business is to be defended only on the ground that the distinctive features of the branch make desirable the recording of its activities in the mechanical framework of a special fund.

The functioning of branch records tends to become an almost autonomous operation of what is practically a completely separate accounting system. Although each branch has a most direct set of relations with the home-office segment of the general ledger—relations that are maintained by carefully integrated systems of reporting and control—each branch tends to function within itself as a completely separate accounting unit so far as accounting processes are concerned. Within the field that it covers, each local ledger and its associated accounting procedures function in large measure as if there were no ties whatever between it and the home-office accounts.

The parallelism of branch accounting and polycorporate organization has been noted by writers and teachers of accounting, and the procedures involved in "consolidating" the reports of the branch and the home office to prepare complete financial statements are quite similar to those involved in the preparation of consolidated statements for an affiliated group of corporations. There may be instances of adjustment of revenue and expense figures, revisions of asset valuation—especially with respect to inventories—and the cancellation of "interdepartmental" items such as receivables and payables, involved in branch reporting as well as in multicorporate reports. The significance of the receivables and payables in the branch records, however, is not at all clear from a personal entity point of view; amounts receivable from customers of the branch are really the legal claims of the parent-corporation, not of the branch, and the obligations incurred by the branch in favor of outside firms are not obligations of the branch but debts of the parent-organization through an agency relation with the branch manager. The legal notion of equities as claims or debts does not coincide with the treatment of these items in branch accounts. Viewing the branch as a "fund" and the obligations of the branch as restrictions upon the assets in the fund, does, however, correspond with the facts of the situation. Branch and factory accounting are examples of the funding of-industrial and commercial accounting, and the principles that have been established in earlier chapters of this discussion apply to such funds.

CONSIGNMENT AND VENTURE ACCOUNTS

Although seldom encountered outside a few specialized areas of business activity, consignments and ventures are examples of funds within funds. Although the accounting is maintained within a single account for each venture, the elements of fund activity are still present. The emphasis in such accounts is upon the maintenance of records that will account for the assets and the restrictions that apply to those assets by reason of the special activities to which they are devoted. It is true that the accounting for operations of this nature is somewhat rudimentary, in view of the fact that a single account is expected to reflect all the details that might appear in a complementary ledger for which the consignment or venture account is the general ledger "control"; but the emphasis upon the special nature of the operations and the consequent segregation of the accounting with respect to them is a clear case of funding, even though the mechanical aspects of fund accounting are reduced or omitted. In fact, sinking-fund and building-fund accounts are of the same general nature as consignment and venture accounts; all these represent the general ledger summarization of what would appear in a complementary ledger if such were actually maintained.

DEPARTMENTAL AND ADMINISTRATIVE ACCOUNTING

The emphasis accorded in recent years to systems of budgetary control and the maintenance of departmental accounts for the purpose of administering the budget have tended to create a fund emphasis in the field of departmental accounting. The operations of administrative units are the basis for various kinds of accounting reports which, although based upon analyses that are perhaps more correctly to be described as statistical than accounting procedures, nevertheless are formulated and prepared within the accounting department and by the accounting staff. Again, here is the recognition of a unit—an entity in the sense of a fund—for which operating reports, budgetary comparisons, and statistical analyses are made. Nor need the unit so recognized be confined to mere grouping of administrative activities; any "center of managerial interest" or "costing unit" may be so treated for specific purposes. For example, a process, a territory, a line of product, method of sale, channel of distribution, characteristic of customers, special order or lot of goods—any of the innumerable ways in which business facts may be arrayed about some salient question or important issue of policy or procedure may form the basis for a statistical tabulation and analysis or a continuing series of reports compiled from data that are collected within the accounting department. Whether or not the procedures are formalized in such a way as to make complete accounting for each of these areas of interest necessary and desirable, the fact remains that for certain purposes various fund entities may be recognized to facilitate the collection, analysis, and reporting of pertinent financial and other data. Thus the notion of a fund outruns the limits of formal accounting and shades off into the statistical tabulation. The notion of a unit for which reports are made—an area of operations around which the collection of facts must center—is a basic element in all quantitative analysis. There need be no personal implications in the choice of such an area of operations; in fact, as the procedures of accounting tend to merge with those of statistics, the legal or personal entity notion disappears because the objectives of the study are more sharply defined, and the questions to be answered are more clearly limned against the related facts. Entity is not a characteristic of a corporation or a business enterprise; it is rather the definition of a purpose to be served, a question to be answered, or a set of data to be marshaled for study and interpretation.

OTHER SITUATIONS

The illustrations that have been presented are not by any means all the cases in which some phase of fund theory has actually been applied in accounting for commercial and financial organizations. The reader can visualize for himself the fund implications in the segregation of principal and income so assiduously maintained in accounting for estates and trusts; the maintenance of not only dollar debits and credits but also "long" and "short" security balances in stockbrokers' accounts; the procedures and the account titles maintained in receivership accounting. All these situations are examples of the use of fund concepts and even certain forms of fund accounts in current accounting practice.[16] The notion of a fund as an accounting unit has gained some degree of usage, even though it may not always be stated in the language of fund accounts. But there is still another area which affords material for analysis and application of fund principles—the phenomenon of polycorporate organization—and this we propose to examine in some detail.

ACCOUNTING FOR POLYCORPORATE ORGANIZATIONS

Probably the closest parallel that can be drawn between the procedural characteristics of fund accounting and the conventional accounts of industrial and financial organizations is the situation of polycorporate organization—the existence of a number of corporations so closely knit together by stock ownership or by other means as to be considered an affiliated group.[17] Here there exists a form of "entity" which transcends the legal bounds of enterprise. The unit for which reports are prepared is one that has no legal personality of its own. Indeed, the only accounts that are maintained in the formal records are separate systems—autonomous and self-sufficing—one for each of the corporate persons. This structure is decidedly similar to the "funds" encountered in other fields; the accounts are established and operated for a separate fund unit covering the operations of each corporation, but the consolidated reports are prepared by combining the data recorded in the separate funds into a more comprehensive presentation—one that might be described as covering the larger fund of which the corporate records are but subdivisions. The "adjustments" and "eliminations" that are made in preparing consolidated statements are entailed by a shift in viewpoint from the fund basis of bookkeeping procedures to the larger fund basis of the polycorporate organization for which reports are prepared.

Although the formality of incorporation lends support to the segregation of records for the individual constituents of the affiliation, incorporation per se is not an essential to such segregation. Consolidated reports may be prepared for any group of related enterprises, regardless of their legal form. The dominant unit, for example, might be a proprietorship, and the subsidiaries might be other proprietorships, simple or complex forms of partnerships, or corporations. The statement has been made that "financial statements presenting a consolidated balance sheet of the affairs of a partnership and a corporation are no more a fiction than corresponding statements relating to corporations only."[18]

As a matter of fact, it is frequently true—especially in the case of closely controlled subsidiary units—that the recording of all the transactions which affect any of the legal units in an affiliation is handled in a single office by a single accounting staff. In such case, the accounting is even more to be regarded as a fund segregation than as a really separate maintenance of accounts for separate legal units.[19]

Other parallels can be drawn between the commercial-industrial affiliation and a fund system of accounts. It is not infrequent that subsidiary companies are established in terms of a functional organization; there may be manufacturing, selling, or financing companies established, or there may be investment companies, property development units, or other kinds of business "departments" recognized in subsidiary corporations. The parallel so often drawn in textbook discussions of consolidated statements between the members of an affiliation and the departments of a single business may be a very real thing. Organization on this basis is almost precisely the same pattern as is generally found reflected in systems of fund accounts.

In the process of preparing consolidated statements, a number of accounting concepts are altered from their conventional content. The notion of revenue, for instance, shifts from the enterprise view to the affiliation view; revenue to a given "fund" in the sense of a single company may not be revenue when viewed from the standpoint of the affiliation. The significance of assets and equities is changed to some extent by the broadening of the fund concept that is employed, and notions of proprietorship and income become decidedly different from those applied to ordinary business situations. In this process, there arise a number of questions and difficulties that cannot be resolved by reference to legal rights and obligations and the legal entities that may be involved.

One instance of this is the definition of the area of consolidation. Moonitz says with respect to this problem:

> It was found impossible, for example, to formulate a workable standard merely on the basis of the size of the parent company's holdings of subsidiaries' shares. Even less objective is the use of "controlling influence" as a guide. Similarity of operations, geographical concentration, and consistency of treatment proved useful as partial standards, but with too many

exceptions and qualifications to warrant isolating them for exclusive attention.

The quest has, however, not been fruitless. Although the exercise of judgment is still essential, the judgment to be made concerns one central inquiry: does an area of integrated operations exist, and if so, where may a definite boundary line be drawn so that all constituent units are included, and those not a part of the enterprise excluded?[20]

The real issue in this situation is that of defining the "fund" that is to be the basis for the consolidated reports. Perhaps this question can never be answered without some degree of arbitrary choice; certainly the definition must depend upon judgment of a number of factors and influences. The fact remains that the consolidated report is based upon something other than legal entities, and the definition of the area of consolidation is an issue parallel to the problem of defining a fund.

Another instance of the fact that legalistic notions have little bearing upon consolidated reports is afforded by the notion of "Consolidated Earned Surplus." This figure is obtained by adding together the net majority interests in the surplus equities as they may be distributed among the companies that are included in the affiliation; but the result is misleading for at least two reasons. First, the figure stated under this caption is only the "majority" or parent-company equity, not the entire surplus as the title would suggest. Second, and more important, the commonly accepted relations between the amount of earned surplus and the amount which might legally be considered available for dividend purposes simply does not apply to the consolidated earned surplus at all. It has been pointed out frequently that dividends could not be declared on the basis of a consolidated earned surplus;[21] dividends are declared by individual corporations upon their specific shares of stock, and the surplus equity that is pertinent to this situation is only that amount which would appear on the books of the corporation declaring the dividend.[22]

A third instance of the fact that legal concepts do not apply to the situation encompassed by the consolidated report is the problem of minority interest. Legally, such words as "majority" and "minority" have no meaning outside the given corporate unit; as the terms are employed in the preparation and presentation of consolidated reports, the problems of applying such terms are quite real. For instance, when two companies operate in the relation of mutual ownership, each company owning 80 per cent of the stock of the other, which 20 per cent equity is the majority, and which the minority interest?[23] Then, too, there are "interests" that fail to correspond with either the majority interest or the minority interest notion, and there is as yet no distinctive term to be applied to these cases.[24] To illustrate, suppose that H company controls P company by ownership of 90 per cent of its common stock; company P in turn owns 80 per cent of S company common shares. The outside stockholders of S company are unquestionably a minority interest, and the stockholders of H company are the controlling or majority interest. The outside stockholders of P company, however, have characteristics of both majority and minority interest; they have a "parental" interest in S company, as well as a direct interest in P company affairs. Even though such stockholders may not be able to wield the power of control,[25] they are not quite in the same position as a pure minority group. This situation may be complicated by the existence of preference shares of one kind or another in one or more of the affiliated companies. In such case the classification of stockholder groups is not a simple division into majority and minority groups. Again, the classification of stockholder interests is at least partly a matter of establishing the area of consolidation; for if consolidated reports are prepared to exclude H company, the position of the outside stockholders of P company would appear to be different—they would be majority stockholders in this case, without qualification. Perhaps the best approach to clear designation of these different stockholder groups is to preserve the company identifications and the specific recognition of the stock interests they represent.

Another group of the problems that stem from multicorporate statements centers around the notion of income as it is affected by the presence of minority interests. Here the legal relationships between stockholders and their companies tend to conflict with the principles that need to be applied to establish such statements. Moonitz recognizes this when he says:

> The position taken here is that a minority interest should not affect the determination of the magnitude of consolidated assets, debts, or total capital . . . . it is recommended that the values assigned be determined without consideration of the size of minority interest. . . . . To permit the value of consolidated inventories and cost of goods sold, for example, to be in part a function of the size of minority interests is to make the resultant magnitudes refer to two entities—the consolidated group and the subsidiary selling the commodities. This is both illogical and unnecessary; for consolidated assets and debts, a minority may be treated in the same manner as a controlling interest, which is tantamount to saying that its existence is ignored.
>
> In the determination of apportionment of consolidated net income and capital, however, the relative importance of the minority may not be ignored.[26]

Here, Moonitz seems to be treating assets, debts, and total consolidated capital as a single fund, and insisting that the valuations should be made of such items independently of the nature of minority interests. Yet he is caught on the horns of a dilemma, with respect to the minority equity, when he says:

> The most direct method of assuring a proper apportionment of net income is to make as many consolidated adjustments as possible against the accounts of the individual companies involved, not against the categories employed in the consolidated reports. For example, if company P holds inventory acquired from its subsidiary, S, at a markup of $15,000, inventory of P and net income of S should be reduced by that amount. The computation of an assumed 10 per cent minority interest in S is then made on the basis of 10 per cent of the net income reported by S diminished by $15,000 of intercompany markups eliminated.[27]

In this case the minority interest is reduced by 10 per cent of the markup, or $1,500, despite the fact that the legal claim of the minority stockholders is unaffected by the consolidation of reports. It would seem that the amount of the restriction placed against the consolidated assets by reason of the minority interest should not be less than the "legal" equity as per the books of the corporation in which the minority shares are held. Yet, if the consolidated assets are written down by $15,000 without changing the legal minority interest, the effect is to reduce the *majority* interest to $1,500 less than the amount that would have been shown, were there no intercompany transaction at all! Does a transaction which is reflected upon the books of a corporation and reported to its (minority) stockholders as a "gain" lose that significance when it is considered in connection with reports of another corporation in which those shareholders have no interest? Or does the recording of such a transaction result in a "loss" to the majority group that offsets the gain to the minority? Moonitz escapes from this dilemma with the following proposal:

> Those who wish to retain in consolidated statements as much information as possible concerning the equity of a minority in a subsidiary's income may do so by incorporating a schedule showing minority interest at subsidiary book value plus or minus consolidated adjustments. In this manner, the amount of "controlled" profit is made available, for whatever the information is worth. . . . . If the minority interest is at all substantial, however, a more satisfactory arrangement is to include the statements of the subsidiary itself as an integral part of the consolidated report.[28]

The real source of this dilemma lies in the fact that, in presenting the equities of the consolidated fund, it is necessary to view the assets from the same point of view. An insistence upon "legal-entity" cost as the basis for inventory valuation cannot support a "consolidated" view of equities. Either the cost concept must be shifted to that of "consolidated cost"—which includes minor equities created by intercompany transfers—or some other valuation base, consistent with the area and the equities represented in the fund, must be established. It should be perfectly clear that "legal entity" theory cannot be applied to consolidated reports without creating problems of this character and that the only basis for solving such problems is to view the consolidated report for what it is: a statement covering the operations of a "fund" that is not the same thing as an aggregation of the constituent parts.[29]

The fact that a consolidated report is not the same thing as an aggregation of the reports of the individual companies which make up the affiliation is further illustrated by the operations involved in the "elimination of the investment account." This expression is an unfortunate one, for what is eliminated is not the investment account but the effects of the acquisition transaction as these may apply to the proprietary equities that appear on the books of the individual companies. The elimination removes that part of the capital stock equity and that part of the surplus equity which existed at the date of acquisition, on the ground that "surplus" should consist only of accumulated "earnings," which so far as majority interests in subsidiary surpluses are concerned, can be recognized only after the date of acquisition. Another way of saying this is that the capital stock and surplus equities which were "purchased" by the acquisition of subsidiary stock are disregarded in the preparation of the consolidated balance sheet. This is neither an entity nor a proprietary concept but a recognition of the fact that in the larger fund area of the affiliation the "investment" in a subsidiary is not an asset to the extent that it represents "purchased" proprietary equities already reflected in the legal statements. By the same token, these proprietary equities do not restrict the asset fund beyond the corresponding amounts shown in the "investment" accounts. Hence, both the asset and the equity elements are removed. To the extent that the cost of the investment is in excess of or is less than the "purchased" equity, there is conventionally shown a "good-will" or "negative good-will" item; this, of course, arises from a cost theory of valuation, not from the nature of the statement, and the resulting good-will or negative good-will is but a "plug" to balance the balance sheet.[30] This may be euphemized by saying that only the parent-company portion of the good-will (that which is paid for by the investment transaction) is recognized in the consolidated statement, but this is reasoning after the fact.

To implement and illustrate some of

the points made in the preceding discussion, and to present the different views that may be held with respect to these points, the following problem situation is presented:

The legal balance sheets of two affiliated companies at December 31, 1945, contained these data:

	Amerc	Britic
Sundry assets	$ 840,000	$500,000
Advance to Britic	100,000	....
Investment in Britic (1,600 shares)	160,000	....
Investment in Amerc (400 shares)	....	100,000
Total	$1,100,000	$600,000
Current liabilities	$ 100,000	$100,000
Capital stock ($100 par)	200,000	200,000
Earned surplus	800,000	300,000
Total	$1,100,000	$600,000

Both investment accounts are carried at cost. Amerc's investment in Britic was made when Britic was incorporated; Britic's investment in Amerc was made January 1, 1933, at which time Amerc's books showed an earned surplus of $200,000, and Britic's books showed an earned surplus of $100,000. Prepare a consolidated balance sheet at December 31, 1945.

Three solutions to this problem will be presented and compared in the following pages. Solution I is based upon the assumption of a "consolidated treasury" and either that the acquisition of Amerc shares was accomplished with Amerc cash or that the Britic company is (for purposes of this solution) reimbursed by Amerc for its acquisition of Amerc shares. This is, of course, at variance with the facts of the case, but the solution is thereby simplified. The treatment of the excess of the cost of Britic's investment over the par value of the shares as a premium on treasury stock has the

SOLUTION I

(Intercompany Investments Are Treated as Treasury Stock)

AMERC BRITIC COMPANIES

CONSOLIDATED BALANCE SHEET AT DECEMBER 31, 1945

Sundry assets	....	....	$1,340,000
Current liabilities	....	....	$ 100,000
Amerc capital stock (par)	$ 200,000	....	....
Less: Treasury shares (par)	40,000	$160,000	....
Britic capital stock (par)	200,000	....	....
Less: Treasury shares (par)	160,000	40,000	200,000
Consolidated surplus:			
Earned surplus, per books, Amerc	800,000		
Add: Amerc equity in earned surplus per books of Britic	240,000		
Gross equity	1,040,000		
Less: Premium on Treasury shares	60,000	980,000	
Britic interest, 20 per cent of the earned surplus per Britic's books	....	60,000	1,040,000
Total equities	....	....	$1,340,000

effect of canceling the surplus equity acquired by Britic in the purchase of Amerc shares along with any possible good-will element, in a single lump sum. Neither the surplus equity acquired nor the good-will is computed separately, and the result ignores any distinction between them. A third feature of the solution is that no attempt is made to apportion surplus accrued after January 1, 1933, other than on the basis of book equities, even though the shares of Amerc acquired by Britic on that date would still have definite rights in the proprietary equities of Amerc until they are retired.[31]

Another approach to this problem involves a separation of the good-will element in the purchase of Amerc shares from the allocation of proprietary equities; further, the surplus increase after January 1, 1933, is divided between the two outside groups of stockholders. The result is:

SOLUTION II

(Good-Will Computed and Shown Separately, and Outside Interests in Consolidated Surplus Computed by Means of Equations)[32]

AMERC BRITIC COMPANIES

CONSOLIDATED BALANCE SHEET AT DECEMBER 31, 1945

ASSETS		
Sundry assets		$1,340,000.00
Good-will from consolidation		4,000.00
Total assets		1,344,000.00
EQUITIES		
Current liabilities		100,000.00
Capital stock, Amerc	$160,000.00	
Capital stock, Britic	40,000.00	200,000.00
Consolidated surplus:		
Amerc portion	947,809.52	
Britic portion	96,190.48	1,044,000.00
Total equities		$1,344,000.00

The shares of the outside stockholders in the consolidated surplus are computed as follows:

Amerc equity (1,600 shares)	
Earned surplus of Amerc, per books, December 31, 1932 . . .	$200,000.00
Amerc share of earned surplus shown on Britic books at this same date	80,000.00
Gross Amerc Company equity in consolidated surplus, as at December 31, 1932	$280,000.00
Of the gross equity, only 80 per cent may be considered in the final consolidated statement, since 20 per cent of Amerc shares were acquired by Britic, at January 1, 1933	$224,000.00
Add: Share of Amerc outside stockholders in the surplus increase from January 1, 1933, to December 31, 1945 (see computations below) .	723,809.52
Total equity of outside stockholders in Amerc per consolidated balance sheet	$947,809.52
Britic equity (400 shares)	
Earned surplus of Britic, per books, at December 31, 1932, was $100,000; of this, 20 per cent applies to outside shares . . .	$ 20,000.00
Add: Share of outside Britic stockholders in the surplus increase from January 1, 1933 to December 31, 1945 (see computations below) .	76,190.48
Total equity of outside stockholders in Britic, per consolidated balance sheet	$ 96,190.48

The equations used to divide the joint increase in surplus of the two companies between the outside stockholder groups are:

$$A = \$600{,}000 + .8B \qquad A = \$904{,}761.90 \qquad .8A = \$723{,}809.52$$
$$B = \$200{,}000 + .2A \qquad B = \$380{,}952.38 \qquad .2B = \$\ 76{,}190.48$$

The good-will shown in the consolidated balance sheet represents the excess of cost over "book value" of the equity acquired by Britic on January 1, 1933; this is computed as follows:

Cost of Britic's investment in Amerc stock	....	$100,000.00
Less:		
20 per cent of capital stock equity of Amerc	$40,000	
20 per cent of the earned surplus shown on Amerc's books at January 1, 1933	40,000	
20 per cent of 80 per cent of Britic's earned surplus per books, at January 1, 1933	16,000	96,000.00
Excess of cost over "book value" (good-will)	....	$ 4,000.00

This item of good-will, however, is not the "parent company's share of the good-will," nor is it the amount of the "good-will acquired by the purchase of Amerc shares." In fact, it is not good-will at all, in the sense in which that term would be applied outside the field of consolidated reports. Ordinarily, accountants consider good-will to be the excess of an entire proprietary valuation over the combined valuations of the net tangible assets of an enterprise; normally, good-will is recognized only as it follows from a bargaining transaction involving the entire proprietary equity or the assets of a business enterprise as a whole.

In this situation there has been no bargaining for entire proprietary equities; there is no addition to the aggregate investment. The real effect of the transaction was to "retire" a portion of the proprietary equity, by withdrawing from "outside" hands a certain block of shares, bringing those shares under the control of the remaining stockholders. The bargaining concerns only a part of the proprietary equity, and the good-will is really nothing but a premium paid to acquire the shares. If there were any good-will to be recognized, it should be that amount imputed to the entire proprietary equity; it is difficult to see, however, how such treatment would be justified in a situation such as this.[33]

The approach to this problem from the viewpoint of fund theory would require that the acquisition of Amerc shares result in no recognition of good-will whatever; if the good-will is recorded at all, it would be written off at once against earned surplus equities. But fund theory would also require a clearer statement of the details of the various stockholder equities. The preparation of a consolidated balance sheet in the given situation of this problem may be presented in a number of separate steps, as outlined.

Step 1.—The consolidated balance sheet as it would have appeared January 1, 1933 (immediately before the acquisition of the Amerc shares by Britic), is shown as follows:

Sundry assets (after elimination of Amerc investment in Britic and deduction of liabilities, if any)		$540,000.00
Proprietary equities:		
Amerc interest:		
Capital stock	$200,000.00	
Earned surplus, unrestricted	200,000.00	
Undistributed consolidated surplus	80,000.00	480,000.00
Britic interest:		
Capital stock (20 per cent)	40,000.00	
Earned surplus (20 per cent)	20,000.00	60,000.00
Total equities		$540,000.00

Step 2.—The effect of Britic's acquisition of Amerc shares may now be reflected in the following *pro-forma* entry:

Capital stock, Amerc	$40,000.00	
Earned surplus, Amerc	43,809.52	
Earned surplus, Britic	190.48	
Undistributed consolidated surplus	16,000.00	
Sundry assets (investment in Amerc)		$100,000.00

This entry records the "retirement" of 20 per cent of the Amerc shareholders' interest, which is simply 20 per cent of that interest, as it appeared in the consolidated balance sheet just prior to the acquisition of Amerc shares. But there is an additional payment of $4,000 (goodwill as shown in the preceding solution) which is in effect a reduction of available surplus as between the stockholder groups.[34] The allocation of this $4,000 is accomplished by use of the equations:

$$A = \$4{,}000 + .8B \qquad A = \$4{,}761.90 \qquad .8A = \$3{,}809.52$$
$$B = .2A \qquad B = \$\ 952.38 \qquad .2B = \$\ 190.48$$

The $4,000 payment, allocated as shown, is viewed as a "retirement dividend" paid to those Amerc shareholders who sold out to Britic; it is viewed as having incidence on Amerc's side, because it is Amerc's shares that are being retired. These charges are added to the others indicated by the 20 per cent portion of those equities that appeared on the preceding consolidated statement.

Step 3.—The transactions which occurred after the acquisition of Amerc shares may now be summarized in the following *pro-forma* entry:

Sundry assets	$900,000	
Amerc equity in earned surplus, unrestricted		$480,000.00
Amerc equity in undistributed consolidated surplus		243,809.52
Britic equity in earned surplus, unrestricted		40,000.00
Britic equity in undistributed consolidated surplus		36,190.48
Current liabilities		100,000.00

The result is:

SOLUTION III

AMERC BRITIC COMPANIES

CONSOLIDATED BALANCE SHEET AT DECEMBER 31, 1945

Sundry assets			$1,340,000.00
EQUITIES			
Current liabilities			$ 100,000.00
Proprietary equities:			
Amerc interest			
Capital stock	$160,000.00		
Earned surplus, unrestricted	636,190.48		
Undistributed consolidated surplus	307,809.52	$1,104,000	
Britic interest			
Capital stock	40,000.00		
Earned surplus, unrestricted	59,809.52		
Undistributed consolidated surplus	36,190.48	136,000	1,240,000.00
Total equities			$1,340,000.00

The computations involved in these items are:

(1) Amerc equity in earned surplus, unrestricted:	
Increase in earned surplus per Amerc books, $600,000; of this, 80 per cent pertains to Amerc shares now outstanding	$480,000.00
(2) Amerc equity in undistributed consolidated surplus:	
Amerc share of combined surplus increase of both companies since January 1, 1933, as per previous calculations	723,809.52
Less: Portion of this reflected on Amerc books and computed in (1) immediately above	480,000.00
Net undistributed consolidated equity	$243,809.52
(3) Britic equity in earned surplus, unrestricted:	
Increase in earned surplus, per Britic books, $200,000; of this, 20 per cent pertains to Britic shares now outstanding	$ 40,000.00
(4) Britic equity in undistributed consolidated surplus:	
Britic share of combined surplus increase of both companies since January 1, 1933, as per previous calculations	76,190.48
Less: Portion of this reflected on Britic books and computed in (3) immediately above	40,000.00
Net undistributed consolidated equity	$ 36,190.48

Step 4.—The final consolidated balance sheet as at December 31, 1945, may be prepared by "posting" the *pro-forma* entries that have been presented to the consolidated balance sheet at January 1, 1933, immediately prior to the acquisition of Amerc shares.[35]

The three solutions that have been presented to this problem exhibit the differences in viewpoint that have been described in the preceding pages of this discussion.

Solution I is based exclusively upon the legal entity view of accounting, even to the extent of assuming that the subject is a "corporation" that includes the activities of the legal units. The consolidated balance sheet is thus viewed as an ancillary report for a *fictitious* company—"a supplementary device, not a substitute for the conventional exhibits of the affairs of either the parent or the subsidiary companies."[36] The calculations are based strictly upon the legal relationships and the legal entities, as transactions are reflected upon their books of account; this is emphasized by the fact that intercompany equities in surpluses of affiliated companies are ignored.

Solution II, on the other hand, is based upon a "proprietary" view of the consolidated report. In this case, the proprietary equities are computed to show the "net worth" of the separate interests, regardless of the specific ties and restrictions that apply to certain portions of the proprietorship because of the legal and equitable interests involved.

Solution III adopts the "fund" viewpoint, and it represents an attempt to apply fund principles (presented in the earlier chapters of this discussion) to the situation at hand. The individual companies are the source of the basic data for preparing the consolidated report, but they are not allowed to influence the viewpoint adopted in the solution. The facts of intercorporate organization cannot be ignored in the preparation of a consolidated report, and, although the fund is not the sum of the corporate activities, it is nonetheless affected by the relationships and the restrictions that arise from the legal structure.

SUMMARY AND CONCLUSIONS

The argument of this chapter has served to demonstrate that the basic notions of fund theory need not be confined to institutions and government agencies. Funds are simply accounting units; they are devised to meet the demands that are made by investors, managers, custodians, beneficiaries, or other people who have some kinds of interest in the tabulations that may be prepared from accounting or statistical records. Despite the fact that textbooks and general writings in accountancy give the impression that the funding of accounts is a practice peculiar to government and institutions, there are many situations in which records and ledger accounts are maintained so as to recognize "fund entities" that may or may not coincide with the legal or even the flesh-and-blood persons who may have interests or connections with the fund operations.

It has been shown that the fund approach to accounting theory may entail some differences in the way in which certain items are treated, especially when there are confusions between legal and economic relationships or when technical difficulties arise in the process of establishing the data that are relevant to a given set of financial reports. These differences, however, are but incidental; the more important conclusion to be drawn is that the basic concepts of fund theory may be applied—indeed, have already to some extent *been* applied—to many kinds of situations. In the subsequent chapters of this monograph some of the implications of fund theory, as it relates to the more common forms of conventional reports, will be developed in detail.

CHAPTER V

FUND-REPORTING AND THE BALANCE SHEET

There has always been a certain difference of opinion as to what a balance sheet is and as to what should be reported therein. The older view, established when balance sheets were employed for purposes of exhibiting or testing the solvency of an enterprise, was that a balance sheet was a statement of financial condition. Later, as it was demonstrated that the accountant could not be expected to portray in such a statement all the necessary forecasts as to financial implications of assets and liabilities, "financial condition" evolved into "financial position," which served to lessen the emphasis upon valuation and value forecasts implied in the earlier notion. One writer, in order to clarify the content of the balance sheet, has even gone so far as to suggest that it represents an accounting for funds received from the shareholders, expenditures for properties owned and benefits unconsumed, retained profits and unexpended funds—a sort of receipts and disbursements statement that summarizes the operations which have transpired since the inception of the venture covered by the statement.[1] The most recent authoritative statement as to what a balance sheet is was formulated by the Committee on Terminology of the American Institute of Accountants in 1941:

> A balance sheet may be defined as a tabular statement or summary of balances (debit and credit) carried forward after an actual or constructive closing of books of account kept by double entry methods, according to the rules or principles of accounting. The items reflected on the two sides of the balance sheet are commonly called assets and liabilities respectively.[2]

This definition amounts to saying that a balance sheet is a postclosing trial balance arranged in a special form, so as to separate "assets" and "liabilities." As an operational definition for the guidance of accountants, such a statement has much to commend it, especially since the terms "assets" and "liabilities" are also defined in similar terms. An asset, in this usage, is

> a thing represented by a debit balance (other than a deficit) that is or would be properly carried forward upon a closing of books of account kept by double entry methods, according to the rules or principles of accounting. The presumptive grounds for carrying the balance forward are that it represents either a property right or value acquired, or an expenditure made which has created a property right, or which is properly applicable to the future.[3]

Similarly, a liability is described as

> a thing represented by a credit balance that is or would be properly carried forward upon a closing of books of account kept by double-entry methods, according to the rules or principles of accounting, provided such credit balance is not in effect a negative balance applicable to an asset. Thus the word is used broadly to comprise not only items which constitute liabilities in the popular sense of debts or obligations (including provision for those that are unascertained), but also credit balances to be accounted for which do not involve the debtor and creditor relation.[4]

Since the word "value" appears in the definition of asset, it may be useful to include this term in the attempt to ascertain what a balance sheet might be:

> Values as used in the accounts signifies the amount at which an item is stated, in accordance with the accounting rules or principles relating to that item. Generally book or balance sheet values (using the word "value" in this sense) represent cost to the accounting unit or some modification thereof; but sometimes they are determined in other ways, as for instance on the basis of market values or cost of replacement, in which cases the bases should be indicated in financial statements.[5]

These definitions may be satisfying to the profession, but they do not serve to make very clear to laymen the meaning and the content of the financial statement to which they refer. From the point of view of an earlier part of the present discussion, these definitions lack "homogeneity of substance" with regard to the uses to which they are applied.

The fund theory would regard a balance sheet as an "inventory statement" applicable to a given fund; it would list the different economic service potentials available for the use of the fund managers (assets), along with the restrictions applicable to those assets arising from the nature of the fund and the operations toward which it is directed. But, since the purposes of a balance sheet are somewhat varied, the term would be a generic one rather than one technically describing some specific statement. The arrangement of the data and the basis for quantifying (valuing) the assets and equities would vary as among the several purposes that might need to be served. For instance, a "balance sheet" for credit purposes would be quite different from other forms. Not only would the valuations be based upon the credit aspects of the case but the classification and arrangement of data would be tailored for this special use. Presumably, the credit statement would be intended to exhibit or to test solvency; thus the assets would be arranged in a form that would stress the ready availability of such assets for realization and liquidation of indebtedness. There would be paired with the expected sources of cash the restrictions that such cash would be required to settle; realizations of assets would be stated in terms of time forecasts, matched with corresponding disbursements on existing indebtedness or outstanding commitments. The result would not be a balance sheet in currently conventional terms; rather, it would be referred to as a "solvency statment." There might even be variations within this theme; solvency may be established with or without reference to projected operations, and it is possible that such statements might be prepared specifically with a view to certain financial plans. Solvency is not a characteristic of assets and equities but the ability to meet obligations as they mature. And, although the balance sheet may be the starting-point for such a presentation, true credit position and solvency depend upon factors that cannot be presented in the extant forms of general purpose balance sheets.[6]

As a report to owners and stockholders—perhaps to some degree also from the point of view of long-term creditors—the balance sheet has a dual significance. On the one hand, it is a report of stewardship, an "accounting" in the legal sense for the assets turned over by equity-holders or those arising from operations not otherwise discharged and reported in operating statements. From this point of view the position taken by Whitney has doubtless much merit; the "charge and discharge" flavor of such a statement is closely associated with the fiduciary nature of the managers' position and with the relationships that exist between them and the persons to whom such a report is directed. But, on the other hand, the balance sheet is a kind of starting-point from which to view the future course of events; the charge and discharge type of statement does not fit this situation at all. For instance, the inventory position of the firm may be good or bad, depending upon the physical and financial data that apply to it. A mere statement of inventory at cost aggregate is no basis upon which to formulate conclusions as to the position of the enterprise, nor forecasts of possible contingencies, upon which to establish investment decisions. Certain supplementary data must be at hand to make the balance sheet useful from this point of view. The exact form in which such data should be presented cannot be answered here with assurance, for there are many considerations that would enter this problem, and much real study of the question would be required to reach significant conclusions. However, we are not so much concerned here with specific forms and methods as we are with underlying theory. The point to be made is that the fund theory would countenance special purpose statements to any extent desired; extant entity and proprietary theories are too much concerned with the question, "*Whose* statement is it?" to consider the problem, "What kind of statement should it be?"

Not only would the fund theory countenance special purpose statements in terms of different arrangements of data and different bases of valuation but it would remove the implication of exhaustiveness in the balance sheet—that is, it would serve to prevent the drawing of inferences that the balance sheet shows all the assets and all the equities, an inference too often drawn by accountants as well as laymen. The argument as to whether the balance sheet includes items that are not assets and excludes some that are[7] arises from the assumption of totality that is implicit in both the entity and the proprietary theories. Every statement of assets is likely to be somewhat incomplete, and every list of equities will be somewhat inaccurate for similar reasons. Assets are sometimes of such nature as to defy quantification in monetary or even in any physical terms; there are things which, although they represent unquestioned assets in some contexts, are not to be so considered in other situations—of what use, for instance, is a patent right or a leasehold from the point of view of going concern solvency, if the realization of this asset would mean the termination of all activities in the enterprise? The partial nature of any financial statement need not be disconcerting to either the person who prepares the statement or the one who reads it, so long as the situation is made clear by specifying the purpose in preparing it and the scope of the fund to which it relates. Trouble arises, however, when financial statements imply an exhaustiveness which cannot be achieved, or which would not provide the needed information if it were! The principal—perhaps the only—requirement that can be applied to a financial statement is that it fit the purpose for which it is intended as well as possible under the limitations imposed by circumstances. So long as it is clear that a statement is a partial statement and that it is aimed at a particular purpose under certain circumstances, no one need object to the fact that the statement does not do more than it claims to achieve. The weakness of present-day balance sheets is that they neither state the purpose for which they are designed nor make clear to the layman the limitations that are involved in them. The answer to this problem might be to educate the public to the conventions of accounting and the underlying difficulties that limit the usefulness of accounting reports; this, however, is a far greater task than to design statements that avoid the implication of simplicity and totality.

One of the most direct and simple ways in which the fund theory may find expression in the balance sheet is in connection with the distinctions that conventionally are maintained between the "current" and "fixed" captions. The separation of these two classes of asset and equity items has become almost universal practice in commercial and industrial reporting; it is a practice that is more or less taken for granted as an underlying tenet of accounting. This classification may, however, be made and maintained in various degrees of formality. Typical American practice has been to make this classification only in the form of groups and subtotals in the balance sheet. In England, however, certain kinds of enterprises are legally required to employ the "double-account form" of balance sheet; in fact, such companies frequently use the "double-account system"[8] of accounting, which involves certain peculiarities that will be considered later. The point to be made here is that the double-account form of balance sheet amounts to "funding" the current and the fixed balance-sheet accounts, so as to report separately the effects of operations upon the current and capital "funds."

The double-account balance sheet recognizes two fund entities in the statement: (1) the current or "floating" assets and equities and (2) the long-term or "capital" items. Dicksee describes this as follows:

> The distinction between the Double Account System and the Single Account System lies mostly in the form the Balance Sheet takes. . . . . In connection with most undertakings is is thought to answer all practical purposet sufficiently well to frame the Balance Sheet as an undivided whole; but with regard to some undertakings, it is thought convenient to divide it into two sections, the first of which comprises "Fixed Assets" and "Fixed Liabilities," along with the balance of the Working Capital; while the second section contains the "Floating Assets," the "Working Capital" and the "Floating Liabilities." Undertakings which divide their Balance Sheet upon these lines are said to employ the "Double-Account System."[9]

The division of the balance sheet into two sections is more than a mere paper arrangement. The idea is clearly evident that the finances of the enterprise are regarded as representing two separate funds. One writer, for instance, says:

> Section 65 of the Companies Clauses Consolidation Act, 1845, provides as follows:
>
> "All the money raised by the company, whether by subscriptions of the shareholders or by loan or otherwise, shall be applied, firstly, in paying the costs and expenses incurred in obtaining the special Act and all expenses incident thereto, and, secondly, in carrying the purposes of the company into execution."
>
> Besides incorporating this, it is the usual practice for the special Act of a company to include a general provision that all moneys raised under it (whether by shares, stock, debenture stock, or borrowing, and including premiums obtained) shall be applied only to the purposes of the Act to which capital is properly applicable. . . . . Thus the Parliamentary company is bound by statutory obligation to make a broad line of distinction between its capital moneys and its revenue moneys, and to keep them on separate accounts and separately applied.[10]

This separation of funds is also apparent in the titles given to the two parts of the balance sheet. The report having to do with long-term assets and equities is entitled "Statement of Receipts and Disbursements on Capital Account," and the current balance-sheet data are listed under the title "General Balance Sheet." The curious fact that the presentation of items in these statements is "reversed" also has some implications. The General Balance Sheet, contrary to American practice, is drawn up with the assets listed on the right side of the statement, and the equities on the left. Whatever may be the explanation for this, however, the Statement of Capital Account is in reverse arrangement to that of the General Balance Sheet, thus conforming to the American practice of showing assets on the left and equities on the right side. The explanation of this curious reversal of arrangement is not clear, but it may well be that, in preparing the statement for the current fund (the General Balance Sheet), the Statement of Capital is regarded as an account with the capital fund rather than a statement prepared by that fund as such. In any event, the reversal of the order of presentation emphasizes the difference of view toward two aspects of what American accountants would consider a single balance sheet.

As opposed to the double-account form of balance sheet, the double-account *system* of accounting differs materially from what is considered modern accounting practice in at least two important respects. The first of these is the treatment of fixed asset costs with respect to expense measurement. Here, the double-account system follows to some extent the pattern described above as representing extant practice in government and institution accounting. That is, the expense measurement with respect to the appropriation of fixed-asset services for current operations is based upon the annual *outlays* for repairs and renewals. The initial acquisition, of course, does not represent an expense of the current fund (as it would under government or institution procedures); rather, such items are reported only as expenditures on capital account. And depreciation, depletion, and amortization of long-term costs forms no part of the double account *system*, as strictly conceived. This is the basis for Dicksee's apparent dissatisfaction with the system, for he says:

> Speaking generally, it is, as has already been stated, a distinctive feature of the Double Account System that it does not provide directly for the depreciation of Fixed Assets. There is, however, no difficulty in employing the Double-Account *form* while yet writing down Fixed Assets to provide for Depreciation; but under such circumstances it is not obvious what advantages remain, as perhaps the greatest advantage of employing the Double Account System at all is that it shows clearly the actual Capital Expenditure that has been incurred upon Fixed Assets from time to time, regarding such figure of cost as being a more useful item of information than any hypothetical valuation of assets which have not been realised, and which it is not intended to realise in the ordinary course of business operations.[11]

From another source, however, we learn that

> to meet this objection [to the lack of attention to depreciation], many companies charge . . . . an average sum against revenue, and credit this amount to a Repairs and Renewals Fund; and after debiting this account with the total expense actually incurred during the period, carry forward the balance as a liability in the General Balance Sheet.[12]

The second major point of difference between the double-account system and extant American practice in commercial and industrial accounting is the treatment of certain receipts and disbursements as capital items per se; as, for instance, "preliminary expense, premiums on shares, etc."[13] The double-account system would treat these organization costs and related items as having no relation whatever to current operations. Thus, organization costs would remain on the balance sheet as a "capital" expenditure (not, it may be noted, as an asset, for capital expenditures are not so captioned) without change throughout the term of operations.[14] The basic philosophy of the double-account system is that capital expenditures are in essence different from current expenditures and are therefore to be kept separately stated regardless of subsequent events. This comes somewhat close to the position advanced by Whitney[15] when he suggests that a balance sheet might be viewed as an accounting for funds handled since the inception of the venture for which the statement is prepared.

The double-account philosophy doubtless had something to do with the conclusions reached in some rather important legal decisions in England. *Lee* v. *Neuchatel Asphalte Company* established the doctrine that "the credit balance of current revenue might be distributed as a dividend without reference to depletion";[16] although this decision was later reversed in America by *Wittenberg* v. *Federal Mining and Smelting Company*, later statutory provisions in almost all recent corporate revisions apply the Neuchatel rule for specified kinds of companies.[17] *Verner* v. *General and Commercial Trust Company* made a distinction between current and capital losses in allowing the distribution of current profits without reference to the shrinkage in market values of stocks held for investment.[18] *Bolton* v. *Natal Land and Colonization Company* established a similar position with respect to shrinkages in land values, and *Wilmer* v. *McNamara and Company* eliminated the shrinkage in good-will valuation from the issue of distribution of current "revenue."[19] In each of these cases there is evidence of distinction between capital and revenue, even though the distinction is difficult to make in the specific case. The double-account form of accounting had a real influence in these cases and upon the legal precedents that still carry weight in English law.[20]

The double-account form of balance sheet and the system of accounting associated with it seem to have been given little attention by American accountants. Some writers, however, have mentioned them with minor emphasis. Hatfield, in a chapter on "Profits" presents the following:

> In England, the discussion has been clearer than in the United States. It has been especially favored by the exceptional form for the Balance Sheet provided for parliamentary companies. The fact that the Capital account is here kept separate, ... seems to encourage the idea that the Capital account or at least the plant purchased with receipts from Capital have little or nothing to do with the profits exhibited in the Balance Sheet. The inference is easily drawn that there can be a loss in the value of capital assets which would affect only the Capital account and which would leave the profits of the year undisturbed.[21]

Esquerré attempted to Americanize the double-account balance sheet; he uses the terms "operating branch" and "financing branch" to distinguish the current from the capital sections of the statement. He writes:

> The profits made by the operating branch are credited to surplus by the financing, and charged to the operating branch when the latter retains them for current needs. As to the operating branch, it correspondingly debits Profit and Loss, in order to close that account, and credits Financing from whom it has borrowed profits.
>
> If the profits are distributed to the stockholders by the financing branch, the account with the operating branch is credited with the amount of liquid assets withdrawn from it to liquidate the debt. Operating, in turn, debits the account with Financing, and credits the asset with which it has parted. . . .
>
> Simple, logical and lucid as it may be, the double-form Balance Sheet is seldom used in America. Its lack of popularity is probably due

to the conviction that the purpose of a balance sheet is to exhibit financial status at any given date, and that the periodical fluctuations of that status are better shown by the statement of income. But, whether or not the double form is used, it remains true that its logical spirit should influence the mechanism of all balance sheets.[22]

It is to be noted that Esquerré, in presenting this Americanized version of the statement, does not give attention to the double-account *system*. Rather, he attempts to fit the double-account form to American ideas of income and avoids discussion of the English procedures.

Kester gave some attention to the double-account form of balance sheet and mentioned the fact that the system of procedures had some influence in the decisions of *Lee* v. *Neuchatel Asphalte Company*, and *Verner* v. *General and Commercial Investment Trust*, stating: "Here, the decisions rested on the distinction between fixed and circulating assets and declared in favor of the maintenance of the capital funds invested in circulating assets, but not necessarily of those invested in fixed assets."[23]

There are only a few other references to the double-account notion in American accounting literature after 1920.[24] But, in 1933, Cole suggested in an article that the double-account balance sheet might be employed to avoid a "burial of the gravestone along with the corpse" in connection with certain types of capital and capital asset transactions.[25] And, as recently as 1940, Paton made the statement in a lecture presented at Harvard University (but without making any additional comment or development of the thought presented) that he thought "it might help our understanding if the practice were revived of dividing the balance sheet horizontally into two sections, the current account balance sheet and the capital account statement."[26]

Although the *Accountant's Index*[27] makes reference to the double-account system in the original volume covering publications through the year 1920, references to this subject do not appear in the index supplements; even Cole's article referred to above is not listed in the index under the subject of double account. Yet the *Accountant's Handbook* continues to show some attention to the subject. The second edition discusses the double-account balance sheet under the caption, "The Sectional Balance Sheet";[28] the third edition shows as one of the illustrative statements a balance sheet of Crompton Parkinson, Ltd., labeled "Analytic Form of Comparative Balance Sheet," for 1937 and 1936.[29] This latest edition of the *Handbook*, however, dismisses the subject of double-account statements with the following:

> Utilization of the device of ruling the "account" and bringing down a balance produces the *sectional type* of account-form statement. Balance Sheets in sectional form are only occasionally encountered in this country, but a two-section statement, generally known as the *double account form*, is sometimes used in English practice.[30]

It is interesting to note that, as the emphasis upon the double-account form declines, the relation between the double-form statement and the separation of capital fund from current fund disappears gradually, until the only relationship recognized is that of "bringing down a balance within the statement." Yet, there are resurgences of the fund emphasis on occasion. George O. May mentioned this form of statement three times in his *Financial Accounting*, in the final reference making this statement:

> The double account system has long been employed in England by companies whose assets are predominantly of a capital nature. Mr. J. M. B. Hoxsey, as a result of his experi-

ence with the New York Stock Exchange, strongly advocated some such form of statement for similar companies in America.[31]

One very interesting variant of the sectional form of the balance sheet appears in a recent company report. The statement shows the current liabilities deducted from the current assets to reflect the net working capital balance; the net working capital figure is treated as one item in the aggregate total of "Net Working Capital and Other Assets." The equities section of this statement is a list confined to long-term and capital obligations.[32] Strictly speaking, this statement is not in double-account form, nor is the associated accounting that of the double-account system; but it does possess the major advantages of the double-form balance sheet. Orthodox forms of the balance sheet are not arranged to show the amount of the net working capital; the importance of this figure for interpretive purposes is good reason for preferring a statement form in which (other things equal) the net working capital figure is displayed prominently. Certain phases of financial policy can be seen more clearly through a comparison of net working capital from year to year than by any other approach; the expansion of a business from funds provided by operations—frequently referred to as "plowing back surplus" (a most uninformative and to some extent misleading term)—can be seen by comparing the shifts in net working capital with income statement figures. The effects of new financing through capital issues or borrowing can be seen in an analysis of changes in the net working capital—which is perhaps one of the reasons for the importance of the "application of funds" statement. Although the fund statement is usually considered to be explanation of balance-sheet changes complementary to the income statement, the idea that the fund statement is an explanation of changes in net working capital has been clearly expressed by a number of writers.[33] The amount of the net working capital is a more significant figure for statement analysis and financial interpretation than any ratio that can be computed from balance-sheet data or any other single figure to be derived from the balance sheet. There are ample reasons for emphasizing this important bit of information in the balance sheet.

Aside from this, however, there are other reasons for preferring the sectionalized statement over a general balance sheet. In the first place, the significance of the current phase of the balance sheet is quite different from the other data presented thereon. The distinction between circulating capital and fixed capital is more than an academic one. It is current assets to which creditors must look for payment of debts and maintenance of credit position, for it is only current assets that represent realizable values that can be depended upon to liquidate claims through the realization of cash; real estate, buildings, patents, leaseholds, good-will, and other fixed assets are valuable only in the indirect sense, that is, their financial significance arises from their use for specific purposes. Markets for disposing of such items are "thin," and prices realized in these markets are largely individual and specialized prices, because these commodities are to a large extent unique goods. More important, the fixed assets generally are of strategic significance to the firm; that is, to dispose of fixed assets of almost any business would mean cessation of operations, because of their over-all importance and of the difficulty of replacing them in parts. As a credit proposition, fixed assets are but a secondary reserve—if indeed they are any kind of reserve fund for the protection of creditors.

From the operating point of view, however, the case is even stronger for the segregation of current items. Profits and losses are almost exclusively related to current funds; losses and gains show up in the current position of the firm, and the transactions that give rise to losses and gains are in large measure transactions that involve current, not fixed, assets and equities. From the financial viewpoint current transactions are significantly related to current assets and equities, both in the number of the individual transactions and in the aggregate amounts involved. And, although an economic view of the situation cannot ignore the significant aspects of fixed capital, the real test of gains or losses from this point of view is to be found in the acquisitions and dispositions of goods and service that are normally and readily available for the satisfaction of immediate wants and needs.

However, there is still another reason for the segregation of current from fixed items in the balance sheet; this has a relation to the problem of valuation. Although we are not here concerned with valuation as such, it is important to recognize that sharp differences exist between the kinds of questions that arise in applying valuation principles to current and fixed balance-sheet items. There are several aspects to be considered; these will be discussed separately.

In the first place, time enters into every valuation in a very significant way, regardless of whether the quantification employed is a cost or a market or even an appraisal figure. Canning pointed this out very clearly when he wrote:

> A direct valuation is possible when, and only when, a realized money income exists and is statistically determinable. . . . . The degree of reliability of such a valuation would be dependent solely upon the reliability of the estimates of amount and time of receipt and outlay and upon the propriety of the rate or rates of capitalization employed.
>
> But it is rarely, if ever, possible statistically to project either the series of receipts or the series of disbursements far into the future. Both series may be substantially completed with respect to such elements as cash, accounts and notes receivable, the liabilities, evidences of debt (of others) held. Both series may be fairly approximated with respect to finished goods inventories. . . . . In some degree both series may be forecast for materials of manufacture on hand, ore deposits in sight, timber stands, etc., but for these the range of probable error in the estimate becomes great.
>
> In a general manufacturing industry, or in any private enterprise holding long-lived assets not for sale but for use conversion, the series of future receipts, *beyond the conclusion of the operating program now in process, becomes indeterminate*.[34]

Two questions are really involved here; one has to do with the nature of the economic services that are being quantified in the valuation, but the other has to do with the money unit itself.

Too often, money is regarded by accountants as well as by other people as the asset par excellence[35]—the most ultimate and objective expression of economic activity. This is to be expected, in view of the fundamental operations in which money plays a significant part—the settling of debts being the over-all expression which covers those operations. Indeed, money is to be regarded as being fundamentally "money of account";[36] it is the established means of expressing debts, prices, and general purchasing power. But this is a description of money, not a concept of it. Money is, in fact, a most abstract and indefinite kind of asset; in terms of the uses to which it is put, and the activities in which it plays a part, money is nothing more than a general unliquidated claim of purchasing power against the over-all market for all goods and services. The only reason for accepting, holding, or using money in any commercial or business sense lies in the fact that money is a general means of satisfying wants, provided that the existing market machinery functions in a normal fashion.[37] The significance of cash is thus merely that it can and may be transformed into various kinds of service potentials at such time and place as the right of choice may be exercised through the usual mechanisms of trade. The meaning of money is thus a momentary one—a function of the series of prices that are extant in the various markets at the given time. Some writers go so far as to point out that the dollar is a most unstable unit, deceptively changing in its significance through time;[38] one accountant[39] has gone so far as to suggest the evaluation of dollar data accumulated from accounting systems through the use of an index of general purchasing power, converting even cash balances to a "common dollar" base. The significance of the money unit itself is bound up with prices and markets, and the time variable is an essential element in the money concept.

Over short periods of time, monetary expressions do have important significance; but over longer periods, at least two factors tend to blur the result of any valuation process. The first is that, as the time period under consideration becomes longer, the significance of the discount factor becomes greater, and the effect of slight differences in the rate of interest involved in the value expression becomes more and more significant. Hence, the valuation of services which involves a long period of time (over which the release and conversion of such services will occur) is subject to error in greater degree than would arise from a short-term situation, because of the effect of differences in the discounting rate. But another and more important element is the "probability" aspect of the valuation.

Every event is conditioned by other events, and a great many different factors may have some effect upon the services ultimately to be derived from a given present embodiment of services. The valuations which arise from the appraisals of future services are only as precise as they may be made by allowance for all those variables that may affect the future. However, there are always more variables to be considered than can be recognized and dealt with in a given case; many of these variables—taken individually—may seem of little importance, though their aggregate and cumulative effect may be quite pronounced. The sample (for it is such) of information upon which the value judgment is based is seldom of such character that one may be sure of the interpretations and inferences that must be drawn; the very conditions which raise the issue of valuation introduce biases which affect the result. But, again, it must be recognized that precision is greater for short-term predictions; the future can always be seen more clearly with respect to short-term commitments than is possible with respect to long-term forecasts. The effects of the many factors that enter the probability side of valuation are less conducive to error over short periods than over long ones.

It should be pointed out that what has been said applies equally well to general market prices and to specific transactions; in other words, it makes no difference as to whether cost, market, or appraisal bases of valuation are preferred in a given situation. For every cost is, at the time of its appearance in some transaction, a valuation; the costs that are regarded by orthodox accountants as the most "concrete"—since they arise from cash exchanges—are at the same time prices in some kind of market situation; they express and are the result of value judgments on the part of those who have had some interest in the goods exchanged. The argument as to the "objectivity"[40] of different kinds of valuations has no bearing on the fact that all valuations are likely to be more reliable—i.e., closer approximations to the actual subsequent events—if they are based upon short-term rather than long-term commitments.

For all these reasons, it would seem highly desirable that the distinctions already recognized in practice between current and long-term items in the balance sheet should not only be maintained but emphasized. Even if the lay reader were informed as to the basis for and the significance of such classification (which is to be doubted rather than assumed), there is still good reason not only to maintain the practice of separating current from long-term items in the balance sheet but also to emphasize it to the extent of recognizing two separate funds and two separate reports. The assets and equities of a given balance sheet do not necessarily and conclusively represent a unitary whole; we have presented on earlier pages examples of many different kinds of "funds" informally or formally recognized as the bases for reports and analyses. It is no great departure from extant procedure to apply the same theory to the balance sheet, so as to separate formally the current and the long-term aspects of given situations. The division of the balance sheet into a "current fund position report" and a "capital fund report" would offer important advantages for clear presentation and better understanding of accounting statements.[41]

The use of the double-form balance sheet is, however, not the whole effect of fund theory upon financial reporting. There are some important implications with respect to operating reports that arise from a fund-theory approach. These, however, are reserved for discussion in chapter vi.

CHAPTER VI

THE FUND THEORY AND STATEMENTS OF OPERATIONS

From the standpoint of conventional financial reporting, the effects of business operations through time are usually considered to be more or less exhaustively reflected in the income statement. One writer, introducing an advanced discussion of the income statement, expresses this view as follows:

> The income sheet is the accountant's historical exhibit. It displays in systematic fashion the results of operations for the period in terms of effect upon earnings—the outstanding point of interest to the active management and to owners and investors, actual or prospective. It is the power to earn profits that is the major characteristic of the going concern as opposed to a lifeless aggregation of assets, and the income sheet is the essential supplement of the balance sheet in this connection.[1]

Notwithstanding the increasing emphasis that is coming to be laid upon "Application of Funds" statements and analyses of reserve accounts in financial reports, it is still true that the great bulk of all financial reports consists of balance sheets and income statements—the first as a statement of position, and the second as a report of operations. In both theory and practice the income statement is considered to be the operating report of major significance; even though supplementary exhibits are presented, the core of all financial reporting is the income statement.

However, the income statement has certain limitations in this role, and these limitations are not to be passed over lightly. A report of the Subcommittee on the Income Statement of the Committee on Accounting Procedure of the American Institute of Accountants presented the following:

> The subcommittee does not . . . . regard the form of the income statement as a problem demanding immediate action to correct serious abuses, but rather as one calling for careful study with a view to making income statements more valuable for the various purposes for which they are used. . . . .
>
> The problem arises out of (*a*) the fact that in part allocations of items affecting the determination of income as between years are necessarily conventional and based on assumptions as to future events that are likely to be invalidated by experience (the items of which this is true, though usually few in relation to the total number of transactions, are frequently large in proportion to the amount of residual income); and (*b*) the disposition of even well-informed persons to attach undue importance to the net income for a particular year.[2]

This statement recognizes that income statements are in fact used for various purposes, and it implies that these different purposes may be served unequally well by any given form of income statement now in use. It also indicates that the problem of income determination is not at all easily solved in view of those few items which must be allocated between periods on the basis of assumptions which are "likely to be invalidated by experience." It seems worth while to examine in some detail a few especially troublesome items with respect to the various purposes that may be involved and the difficulties of measurement that are encountered in the allocation of costs and revenues to specific fiscal periods.

It is obvious that income statements are handled and read by a great many different classes and kinds of interested parties. However, the important fact—even though it may not be quite so obvious—is that there are a number of different concepts or points of view as to the *meaning* of income. The most direct instance of this is afforded by the fact that bondholders and preferred and common stockholders each view the given income statement differently. The fairly common practice of showing subtotals in the income statement "before interest," "before federal taxes," "available to preferred dividends," and "available for common shares" is tangible evidence of a recognition of these different points of view. Yet it does not mean at all that the bondholder is not concerned with the amount of federal taxes or preferred and common dividends; after all, much of the security behind a given bond issue is the ability to continue operations in such form as to continue the payment of preferred and common dividends. The bondholder's interest is different from that of other security-holders, not in the sense of being opposed to such interests, but simply in terms of a viewpoint that is not the same. All the security-holders are interested in an income figure that may be employed as a basis for forecasting the future welfare of the firm, but the emphasis is to be given certain data and the kinds of data that are relevant to specific investment decisions are not the same for all cases.

Quite distinct from this viewpoint is the one taken by management. Management is interested in historical reports as a basis for evaluating the accomplishments of the period against the potentialities of the future. Much of the data with which management is concerned are of the type that simply cannot be presented adequately in the income statement; yet to the extent that income statements are used by management, the viewpoint is decidedly different from that of any one of the security-holders. It is not a breach of ethics to present management with information different from that prepared for investors; it is rather a recognition that data which will serve one purpose well do not necessarily have significance for other situations. The very form of the income statement as it is conventionally prepared suggests that the data thus presented are not "all the facts, nothing but the facts"; this is because facts are themselves generalizations and interpretations rather than mere physical phenomena. This is not lost sight of in the preparation of orthodox statements, but the view that is taken is frequently that of "general purpose" information, which does not meet the needs of any one of the interested parties in the way that it should.

A second phase of this situation may be observed in the effects of recent federal tax policy. High rates of income and excess profits tax have served to emphasize the notion of "tax savings" as a factor in managerial decision; it has also raised a number of issues as to the allocation of tax charges and tax savings both between periods of time and as among various sections and items shown within the conventional income and surplus statement. Some of the issues tend to confuse the meaning of cost itself, when certain transactions have the effect of reducing the tax liability for the period; and, when the allocation of tax charges and credits is attempted, there arises the somewhat complex question of whether or not the total average tax rate or the marginal rate in the highest bracket should be employed for the purpose of allocation. There are no answers to questions such as these except in terms of a given context of other data and with a view to the purpose involved in the analysis. It is not at all surprising to find that, as this is written, two authoritative bodies seem to be at loggerheads as to what should constitute adequate financial reporting in this general area of federal tax effects.[3] This little problem is but a phase of the general situation which illustrates the difficulty and the weaknesses involved in the preparation of orthodox income statements to report operations.

A third phase of the problem of income reporting as it impinges upon the various uses of income statement data has to do with so-called "equalization reserve" procedures. It is a moot question whether the income concept (and the income statement as an expression of this concept) is not open to serious limitations in situations which call forth the "equalization reserve" procedure. Paton takes a decided stand against equalization reserves as they apply to several fiscal periods, though he is willing to have them used within a given fiscal period. He writes:

> An operating reserve used in allocating to particular months annual expenditures for advertising, for example, may have either a debit or a credit balance at interim points, and while a debit balance can be interpreted as a form of prepayment it seems a bit far fetched to view a credit balance either as an offset to working capital or a liability. Perhaps the best solution, if a definite decision is required for balance sheet purposes, is to view a credit balance as a short-run adjustment of surplus. It should be added that the use of equalization reserves to spread charges in monthly or quarterly reckonings in terms of an annual budget, with a closing out of the reserve at the end of the year, is not objectionable practice, whatever may be the merits of long-run apportionments. . . . .
>
> There is serious doubt as to the propriety of any scheme of charging operations with estimated average losses due to fire or other casualties. . . . . A serious objection to the accruing of reserves to cover possible casualties by means of charges to revenue or income, coupled with the practice of charging actual losses to such reserves as they occur lies in the misleading income statements which result. The substitution of hypothetical charges for actual losses at the best brings about an artificial smoothing of yearly figures and at worst leads to downright understatement of income over a long period.[4]

This view would seem to condemn the averaging or spreading of such charges over the years. Yet it cannot be entirely denied that for some purposes at least "income" must include some average charge for this class of losses. This is certainly true, if the income figure is to be used as a basis for forecasting future fortunes of the enterprise. And it should be noted carefully that the omission of reserve procedure tends to make the actual charges (when losses do occur) fall into the category referred to in the Institute subcommittee's report—items of a size large relative to the balance of reported net income that may be prorated only with difficulty. The basis of "actual" reporting of such losses without the reserve procedure would emphasize the need for viewing a series of income statements over some period of time to permit a normal view of the situation. Yet if a period of years were chosen which would be long enough to show the losses in question in proper perspective, it is quite possible that this period would reflect also some changes in operating conditions and management factors which would make the long-run comparison weak, perhaps useless; the forces of economic, managerial, or technological change might be such as to bias the rest of the income data more than enough to offset any possible gain from averaging actual rather than "equalized" charges. This phase of the accounting problem is simply another instance of the fact that income data are not the same things when viewed for different purposes.

A fourth limitation in the typical income statement is afforded by the distinction—already well intrenched in the control procedures of internal accounting system—between fixed and variable costs. There is a difference, from some points of view, between costs that tend to follow changes in the rate of activity and those which do not, or which do so but imperfectly and with certain lags and differences. There is even some reason to suspect that the position taken by some accountants—that "in their essential relation to revenues, as in their essential relation to assets, all costs are homogeneous and rank abreast"[5]—is open to some discussion with respect to fixed charges as these affect inventories and expense.

The first aspect of this situation is evidenced by the fact that one writer has proposed a realignment of the income statement so as to separate variable from fixed costs in the presentation. The case is presented in the following terms:

> The measure of managerial accomplishment is not the net profit earned by the department after all costs, both variable and fixed. The significant figure is the department's contribution to general overhead; that is, the balance of revenue after deducting those variable costs which are *actually caused by the operations for the period*. . . . . It is proposed that a somewhat similar classification of costs be used in the operating section of the income statement.[6]

Another writer stresses the need for separating fixed and variable costs but raises, in addition, the question of allocation of fixed costs to fiscal periods. In an analysis drawn up in the form of an income computation he shows the item "fixed manufacturing expense lost through non-use," and he writes:

> Neglect to make a clean-cut distinction between fixed and variable expenses of manufacturing, or an inept attempt at their separation, or, worse still, the omission of the fixed expenses from the costs injects error into the accounts of services, of processes and of job-lot burden which may well affect the judgment of management in its attempts to control costs and efficiency. If this neglect or ineptness of cost accounting means that no distinction between costs of utilized facilities and losses on idle facilities is made, the inventories are misstated on the balance sheets and the costs of goods sold and the losses resulting from the non-use of facilities are misstated on the profit and loss statements.
>
> The reasoning involved in the foregoing statements is not original with me, but I concur fully in the conclusions. That more of the operating profit is left for net income because more of the facilities were utilized by increased production without an increase in sales, seems to me to be a fact well established by reasoning; that some accountants object to this fact and suggest manipulation of the cost accounts to avoid it, with accompanying violation of the truth relative to the costs of the goods sold, to the costs of inventories, and to the net income retained seems to me to be unnecessary, to put it mildly.[7]

However, this writer goes on to point out that the controversy may be more important than a simple disagreement, for he says:

> Is it not possible that the error lies in the inflexible form of the profit and loss statement and in its interpretation rather than in the reasoning of either party to the controversy? It seems to me that our neglect or failure to evaluate the effects of artificial periodicity on the statements of profit and loss and on other phases of accounting is the cause of many of our disagreements. Perhaps it may be so in this case; or perhaps it is but a quirk of human nature that leads us to search the other man's field for our lost ox before searching our own.[8]

A fifth difficulty with the conventional form of income statement involves distinctions between gains and losses which arise from specific transactions and those which are the result of price changes;

that is, the separation of price-change effects from transaction gains and losses. This, of course, involves some aspects of valuation procedure; the proponents of last-in-first-out methods of inventory pricing have made much of this point.[9] The fact that apparent gains and losses may arise either from mere changes in prices over some period of time, or from differences in the current significance of economic changes, is recognized by accountants generally; but not much progress has been made toward separating those effects in financial reports. This is partly because of the traditional emphasis upon a single income figure as a report of operations for a given period. So long as the basic question of financial reporting is tied to the income notion, the problem of separating price profits from transaction profits appears academic, because the test that is applied is framed in terms of whether or not the effect in question is to be recognized in the income figure.

However, to make a forecast of future expectations (as present or prospective investors must do in making their decisions) from an income statement in which price fluctuation effects are not shown separately is nothing short of foolhardy; such a procedure assumes implicitly that the price patterns of the immediate past will be repeated and perpetuated in the future. Even the use of a series of income statements is open to serious error under such conditions, unless the price changes which have occurred may be assumed to be insignificant or may be thought to average out. The first assumption is seldom a safe one to make; the dynamics of the price system constitute an essential part of the risk element in any business venture that involves holding assets over a period of time in which prices may change. The second assumption is invalid unless the series of income statements cover precisely one price cycle—even then there remains to be considered the effects of shifts in inventory commitments over that cycle. The fact that business management does in practice strive to some degree to anticipate price changes, increasing or decreasing inventory commitments in response to those anticipations, makes the shift in inventory position over the cycle an important factor in profits.

When issues from inventory are priced on a first-in-first-out basis during a period of rising replacement costs, the effect is to bury "price profits" in the "cost of goods sold" and the aggregate income figure. Following the principle of lower of cost or market on a downswing of replacement costs loads the income statement with price losses of considerable size. If the lower of cost or market principle is not followed on the downswing, there is still an element of price loss buried in the cost-of-goods-sold figure as the higher prices near the peak of the cycle get into the issues from inventory. On the other hand, the use of last-in-first-out methods tends to *exclude* the effects of price fluctuations from the income statement; the only price effects that do get into the income calculation under last-in-first-out procedures are those covered by actual withdrawals from stores; even then, they appear only to the extent that normal inventory quantities are reduced, or the time lag between purchases and issues becomes appreciable. The resulting difference in the amount and the timing of income are reflected in the margins between the alternative valuations (first-in-first-out versus last-in-first-out) of the initial and final inventories for the period or periods in question. These differences—from the point of view of the proponents of last-in-first-out—measure the "unrealized price profit or loss"; they are included in "income" under first-in-first-out procedures but excluded from income under last-in-first-out methods. It should be emphasized that both methods really *ignore* the "unrealized price profit or loss" in different ways: the one "ignores" it by burying the effect in "income" without explanation, the other "ignores" it by excluding it from any computation of income or other financial data, also without explanation.

The real issue involved is not how this element should be *ignored* but whether it should not be segregated as an important element of financial significance in the operating reports, and mentioned explicitly, as an aid to the formulation of financial judgments on the part of those who read financial statements. If there is a difference between a realized and an unrealized gain, the distinction should be made clear by specific reporting, and the "unrealized element of income" should be measured as best it can. There are cases in which the information concerning unrealized appreciation in inventories is indeed essential information. When large inventories have been built up by following a policy of speculative purchasing at the lower levels of the price cycle, an upward swing of prices represents a material change in the significance of the inventory; holding large amounts of material acquired at prices materially lower than the current replacement cost at the date of the financial report may be a strategic factor in the financial condition and the forecast of future operations. So long as prices remain at or near the current (higher) level, the presence of such an inventory situation means that cost savings can affect materially the future income to be expected when this inventory is released to operations.

Not only do current forms of financial reports fail to point out this factor, but, when price changes are drastic (e.g., in the rubber industry in 1927–32), the balance sheets may actually show decreases in inventory from year to year through lower of cost or market valuations, when physical inventories have been expanded to far above normal levels, and the price advantages thus gained are of the highest importance to subsequent operating results. Comparisons of first-in-first-out with last-in-first-out valuations would not reflect this situation adequately, for, unless inventories are "turned over" continuously (carrying amounts in physical units equal to or less than daily rate of issue), there is a lag between price changes actually affecting current purchases and the prices charged on inventory issues. This lag becomes greater as inventory balances are increased through heavy purchases; it is decreased as purchases fall below the rate of issue from inventory to operations. In a case such as the one mentioned, this lag may become quite considerable; as it becomes larger, the measure of "unrealized price profit or loss" as established by comparison of first-in-first-out with last-in-first-out valuations is biased, showing less than the theoretical appreciation in periods of rising prices and more than the theoretical declination in periods of falling prices; and there are mixed effects at the peaks and troughs of the price cycle, depending upon the physical size of inventory.

But however it may be measured, the price effect—at least to the extent of "unrealized price profit or loss"—should be shown explicitly somewhere in the financial reports. Whether or not the price effect may be separated for transactions that are completed through sale and delivery is a statistical problem of some dimensions which would doubtless involve certain compromises in the interest of expediency;[10] the problem is, however, somewhat beyond the limits of the present discussion.

The more pertinent observation to be made is that the discussion of such subjects—and research and action toward meeting such problems—are hampered by the traditional view that the income statement is *the* operating report, and the measurement of income is *the* great responsibility of the accountant. The reporting of financial data might proceed with much more effectiveness if thinking did not need to be channeled through questions of whether or not a certain item constituted income, when there is no one concept to which the "income" label may be applied exclusively.

As a last group of items to illustrate the limitations of income statements in the role of operating reports, attention is called to the data that are ordinarily characterized under the captions of "capital gains and losses," "adjustments or corrections of income for past periods," and "provisions for special purposes" which commonly appear in the lower sections of the conventional income statement or as "surplus adjustments" in the statement of surplus. These items make up a considerable part of what the subcommittee report on the income statement characterized as being "usually few in relation to the total number of transactions" but "frequently large in proportion to the amount of residual income." Some of these items are of the nature of nonrecurring transactions; and, as such, they should be reported separately from other income-determining factors; for some purposes nonrecurring items are of importance, whereas for some other purposes they are irrelevant. The trouble is, however, in establishing whether certain items are in fact in this category. Capital gains and losses arising from holding securities and investments over long periods of time may be sporadic as to their appearance in the income statement, but they cannot be considered to be nonrecurring items in the strict sense, so long as investment in stocks and bonds is one phase of the operations covered by the financial reports. To the extent that this is so, capital gains are more nearly like the second classification, "adjustments or corrections of income for past periods." It is this class of special items that gives much difficulty in presentation and interpretation of an income statement; their inclusion is, of course, necessary, yet they do not add much to the meaning of a series of income statements except uncertainty. If the income statement purports to present a computation of income, the presence of such adjustments and corrections can only reduce the effectiveness of the presentation; yet they must be shown if the ultimate effect of the income presentation is to be at all correct. If the income statement is what it purports to be, such adjustments should be set up to show the allocation of the charge or credit to specific income periods; income loses much of its meaning if the time period involved is not understood. If this is not done, the averaging effect of reading a series of income statements in which such items appear may actually produce an erroneous impression as to the effect of such items on the income picture.

A certain amount of loose terminology also appears in dealing with items of this character. One instance is the item of "gain or loss on the retirement of fixed assets"; it is seldom possible to establish how much of such an adjustment is really a "gain" or a "loss" and how much represents correction of unavoidable errors in estimating depreciation, depletion, or amortization charges in past periods. It would be better to describe such an adjustment for what it is rather than to suggest that the disposition of fixed assets is a source of income or loss.

Even more confusing are those special provisions for contingencies or probable future effects of certain combinations of events. The handling of estimated tax savings with respect to pension plans is an illustration; another is afforded by the specific instance that appeared in the annual report of one corporation: the operating report of profit and loss and earned surplus for 1938 showed an addition to the surplus for the current year of $4,000,000 carried to the current report from a "Material and Products Price Equalization Reserve." The president's letter accompanying this report stated:

> In addition to this continuing market loss throughout the year, the Company, at the close of the fiscal year on June 30, in accordance with good accounting practice, wrote down the book value of its entire inventory on hand in the amount of $3,802,810.93, thus reducing it to the lower of cost or market.
>
> The Reserve for Material and Products Price Equalization was created in prior years for use in a contingency such as this, in order that the amount available for dividends in a year wherein the earnings were adversely affected by declining markets might be somewhat equalized. This reserve was reduced during the year just ended from $4,700,000 to $700,000.
>
> The prices prevailing on June 30, 1938 were relatively low, so that no larger Reserve seems to be warranted at the present time; however, should prices advance, it would seem to be sound procedure to rebuild this fund [*sic*] as opportunity offers, and maintain it on some basis in keeping with the level of market values.[11]

Except for a qualification as to the use of reduced depreciation rates which calls attention to the fact that depreciation charged was $560,000 less than it would have been with the prior year's rates, the auditors' statement in this report is not unusual, even to the stereotyped "in accordance with acceptable principles of accounting consistently maintained by the companies." What this annual report does not show is that the bulk of this equalization reserve was created by a single charge to "income" in 1936; incidentally, the remaining $700,000 of this reserve was "transferred to income" in the next ensuing year. Even if the reader of financial reports may be assumed to understand the real significance of reserves and transfers of this kind, practices such as these are disconcerting, to say the least. But to use such an approach to financial reporting in a statement that purports to show an "income" computation for the consumption of an uninitiated reader is nothing short of being downright misleading!

In considering the problems and practices of income reporting, it is worth keeping in mind that the layman's conception of accounting income is not always a technically adequate one. Far too frequently the layman will assume that the accountant has done his work for him and that the final figure is the important one for his purposes, when the chances are good that nothing could be farther from the truth. The fact that income is frequently confused with cash balances is not the fault of the accountant, but it is a fact that the accountant should guard against in every possible way; the easiest and most effective way to do this is to abandon entirely the notion of a "general purpose" income statement and to force a reading of the entire financial report simply by abstaining from any reference or suggestion of an income computation in overt form. This, as we shall see, need not involve the withholding of any essential facts; indeed, it may result in the possibility of presenting more data, and those more effectively than is possible with extant forms of financial reports.

One of the principal sources of difficulty for the accountant is that, because of conventional emphasis upon income, he is forced to consider the "income" effect of whatever data he may wish to present. To show an unrealized appreciation in an operating report necessarily implies a relevance of this item to the income computation; and, since there are no simple means of reflecting such information without suggesting an income relationship, such data are "justifiably" withheld from the reports. However, were the accountant released from the strict and confining patterns of formal income statements, he might report many things of importance that must now be buried or eliminated in preparing the financial statements. As it is, the most realistic statement that can be made about the income figure so prominently displayed in the reports is the statement made by Canning: "What is set out as a measure of net income can never be supposed to be a fact in any sense at all except that it is the figure which results when the accountant has finished applying the procedure which he adopts."[12]

But this is not, however, the entire case with respect to the limitations of income statements as reports of operations. In terms of its very mechanics, the income statement is too narrowly conceived to be really useful in portraying the effects of operations. All the conventional income statement can show is the *gain or loss effect* of transactions; there are many transactions of considerable importance which, because they involve no gain or loss, cannot be included in an income statement. Thus it is that the statement of funds enters the field of financial reporting procedure. We shall have reason to consider the statement of funds in some detail at a later point in this chapter.

Solutions proposed for the problems raised by the limitations of the income statement are worth considering here, for they indicate just what kinds of issues are really involved in the problems. The subcommittee on the income statement made the following suggestions:

> The subcommittee believes that efforts should be directed to the following objectives:
>
> First, to educate the investing public to attach less importance to results of a single year, and to consider, rather, the results of a series of years;
>
> Second, to encourage the practice of drawing attention to items which have been excluded from the income for the period, whenever figures of net income or net income per share are presented to investors;
>
> Third, to determine what general concept of net income for the year is most practically useful;
>
> Fourth, to define as clearly as possible conditions under which items might be excluded from the ordinary section of the income account and included in either a special section or in surplus.[13]

These are probably as good a set of suggestions as could be made with respect to the problem of income reporting, but they do not and cannot offer satisfactory means of dealing with all the issues in the problem. The first suggestion is a good one, in the sense that a real education of the public would achieve a large measure of success in dealing with the problem. But education is a long, slow, and tedious process; it must involve a change of thinking on the part of the educated, and this implies an effort on the part of the public to be interested in technical patterns of thought. Such an effort can be called forth, if at all, only by comprehensive and intensive educational programs. Unless the education aimed to disseminate a full understanding of the accounting process and its problems, it could not hope to go far. Such an educational objective, while interesting to contemplate, is far too ambitious a goal to be realized within the limits of available resources in any short period of time; in addition, the cost of such a project or program would be prohibitive. Education of the public is desirable and should be striven for, but it is not a very satisfactory solution to the problem of how financial data should be reported to people who "do not like" to analyze accounting reports.

The second suggestion is also meritorious, but one cannot always be sure as to just what items should be brought to the attention of those who read financial statements. Unfortunately, the suggestion implies that there now are excluded certain data that should be reported to investors; if the statement is to be taken at its face value, it merely emphasizes the point made above—"income" emphasis creates difficulties in financial reporting simply because everything shown in an income statement must be related to "income."

"To determine what concept of income is most generally useful" is futile; uses are specific, not general! And, while errors may be shifted in changing one general concept for another, the same problem still persists with *any* general-purpose figure. Canning's statement applies with full force to any general purpose computations:

> To adopt uncritically data drawn from general purpose reports of the accountant in the study of any financial problem of public character is as dangerous logically as to conclude from the fact that a particular index number of wholesale commodity prices has risen, that the cost of living in a particular community has risen correspondingly.[14]

To present an income figure aimed at some "most generally useful" purpose puts a burden of interpretation upon the accountant that he ought not to assume. Of all the various ways in which income statement data may be employed, and with all the different meanings and applications of the income computation, there is hardly any one that can be assumed to be of "most practicable usefulness." By the very act of making up *any* income statement, the accountant presents some one concept of income which —with all due respect to the ability that may be displayed and employed in the process—can hardly be expected to fulfil all the important demands that will be put upon it. No matter how the general purpose figure is defined, it will still be a single amount, a single computation fit for only a single use. And it should also be emphasized that the demands for data cannot be met by subtotals or partial calculations, unless the purpose to be served can be related to such subtotals. What is needed is not a new mold for income calculations but a new and more flexible means of presenting operating data.

The last proposal—that definitions be framed to distinguish various sections of the income statement and the surplus account—is one that does not appear to be too fruitful in its potentialities, in view of the trends toward adoption of "combined statements of income and surplus" and "single-step" income reports.[15] Even so, this would meet but a part of the difficulties and limitations of the income statement as a report of operating results.

The basic restriction upon the usefulness of an income statement is that, although the items reflected within it arise from and are related to changes in assets and equities, the income statement views these transactions only as they may affect the residual equity of owners, or the relations between owners and managers of a business firm. The whole statement is set in a framework which emphasizes "gain or loss" aspects of transactions, exclusive of other considerations. Nor does it seem to change the picture very much if the proprietary view of accounting is contrasted with the entity position. In a discussion of "conceptions of business income," Paton contrasts the proprietary and the "managerial" (entity) views:

> According to the first of these, periodic net income or profit is the amount accruing to the owners in the narrow sense—sole proprietor, partners, or stockholders—as a result of the existence and the activity of the enterprise (and net loss is similarly interpreted). This is the traditional view in accounting, and corresponds substantially to the conception employed in determining income for tax purposes and in other connections dominated by legal considerations. It emphasizes the controlling, residual interest rather than the enterprise as a whole, and does not encourage classification of deductions into expenses, losses, and contractual income distributions. In the case of a corporation with two or more classes of capital stock, it should be noted, there are corresponding subdivisions of proprietary profit.
>
> The managerial conception stresses the business as an economic entity and interprets income, accordingly, as the return earned by the entire fund of capital employed, regardless of source. To the operating manager, concerned with effective utilization of all the resources at his disposal, there is no distinction between proprietary contributions and funds furnished by creditors. Net income from this standpoint is the excess of revenue over all charges assignable to such revenues as costs, before consideration of interest or other distributions to those who have furnished capital to the undertaking.
>
> In recent years the managerial point of view has been increasingly emphasized by accountants, especially in the field of cost accounting, but the proprietary conception has continued to be more influential in the preparation of general income statements. It needs to be recognized that both approaches are entirely valid in particular areas, and that in good income reporting both are fully reflected in the classifications employed.[16]

It would seem from this statement that there is really but little difference between the proprietary and the entity viewpoints so far as the income statement is concerned.[17] Although there are some aspects of accounting that are treated differently under the two systems of thought, the income statement would appear to be the same under either view, except as to the number of items that are to be recognized before "income" emerges in the statement.

THE STATEMENT OF FUNDS

Another view of the problems of financial reporting is afforded by the statement of funds. Not only does the statement of funds itself point up some of the limitations of the income statement, but it also offers some basis for a different approach to the problem of presenting certain kinds of financial information. The importance of the statement of funds is gradually increasing, and there is good reason for this; the statement of funds serves a need not met by any other form of financial report. One writer says:

> The so-called "statement of funds" is an important technical means bringing to light underlying financial operations and movements—the ebb and flow of forces in terms of major elements and factors—which are not directly revealed in reports of the balance sheet and income sheet type, no matter how carefully prepared and arranged. This statement is used, in other words, to assemble in systematic form the essential effects and results of all transactions and operations for a given

period—usually one year—upon the primary financial sinews of the enterprise.[18]

In a series of lectures dealing with "Improvement in Financial Accounts," George O. May stated: "Another valuable form of statement which might well be more generally adopted is the summary of resources and their disposition, such as the United States Steel Corporation has for many years published."[19]

Statements of funds have been employed to further comprehensive economic and financial studies; Moonitz mentions a number of analyses of this character in which statements of funds were employed.[20] There seems to be an observable tendency for more and more public accountants to include statements of funds in their audit reports,[21] and one company has even gone so far as to set up a twenty-year comparison of "Sources and Dispositions of Working Capital" (thirteen of which are shown in detail) so as to present a historical picture of the "ebb and flow of values" from the incorporation of the firm.[22]

Despite the growing acceptance of the fund statement as a basic form of financial report, there is still considerable confusion in the literature of accounting as to the content and the purpose of this report. The reasons for this are difficult to establish, but the fact is that the statement of funds has developed—like many other accounting procedures and concepts—largely from the exigencies of practice; and little has been done in the way of establishing the theoretical basis for such statements. As we shall see, fund theory does offer a consistent and logical position for the fund statement among accounting reports and recognizes an important function that is served by this statement. However, this is a story of some length, and it had best be told from the beginning.

Most writings on the subject of the fund statement[23] begin by observing that the statement is prepared from comparative balance-sheet and income-statement data; that the fund statement deals with "net" items only (whatever that may mean!); and that, for one reason or another, the effects of certain kinds of transactions are ignored in the fund statement. Seldom is any express attempt made to define "fund" as a term; if the definition is attempted at all, it is usually allowed to degenerate into some rough-and-ready approximation of "cash," sometimes despite a previous observation that the statement is not concerned with cash receipts and disbursements.[24]

Some writers state categorically that the fund statement deals with cash items; one writer says:

> For the application of funds summary, if the best purposes are to be served, the word "fund" should be used as practically synonymous with "cash." By "practically" we mean that an application of funds summary does not have to be as *accurate* as a statement of cash receipts and disbursements.[25]

Other presentations leave the reader in some confusion as to what is meant by funds and what (if anything) the fund statement could have to do with them:

> . . . . The Fund Statement is useful in summarizing the changes which have taken place during the accounting period in the balance sheet items in so far as they reflect the flow of current funds through the business. The term "funds" is similar to "cash" but it is somewhat broader; it is much like the concept of invested capital. The opening balance sheet of a corporation might well be called a fund statement and it could be presented in the form of such a schedule.[26]

Another statement that exhibits the same kind of confusion is:

> Probably the most difficult thing for businessmen to comprehend when analyzing finan-

> cial statements is the fact that the cash of the business does not usually increase in direct proportion to the profits earned. It is difficult for them to understand why their cash is low, or why the working capital has not increased when it is known that a profit and perhaps a large one has been earned. The statement of funds—sources and applications has been developed to provide the explanation for the changes in the amount of funds during a given period. . . . . It is not feasible to attempt to trace the course of all funds. . . . . A statement of cash receipts and disbursements may be prepared, however.[27]

Even those who, from a background of broad experience in accounting and financial reporting, recommend the extension of use of the fund statement are not too careful to make clear its function and the content:

> The statement of resources and their disposition answers the vital question,—what has become of the cash?—and affords a useful corrective to views formed on the basis of an income account which perhaps unduly emphasizes net earning capacity as distinguished from net current receipts of income.[28]

The fund statement is definitely and clearly related to the kind of balance-sheet presentation that was described in the preceding chapter. In fact, the statement may be described and related to the balance sheet in those terms. By "funding" the balance sheet, treating it as if current assets and current equities constituted a separate fund, the amount of the net working capital is stated explicitly. To show this figure explicitly is to call attention to changes in it from year to year; such changes would inevitably give rise to an analysis or a report to explain those changes.[29] The function of the fund statement in such case is not to bridge the gap between income and cash or to summarize important transactions reportable in no other way; rather the fund statement reports those transactions which affected the residual equity in the current fund. This view has more to commend it than appears at first glance.

In the first place, the fund statement would have a definite beginning and a definite end. The current residual equity would be stated in the current balance sheet at two dates; the statement would begin with the first and end with the second balance. Such an arrangement of the statement would serve to tie the fund statement into the balance sheet in definite terms, and the progression of ideas in the statement would be logical and complete. There need be no emphasis upon the usual "total funds provided" or "total funds applied"—these totals are, as a matter of fact, meaningless as well as unverifiable, because the fund statement does not deal only with cash transactions.[30]

Second, the problem of handling certain kinds of transactions in the fund statement is simplified by the approach we are taking. The case of a dividend declared but not paid is an example of this. The declaration of a dividend is an alteration in the form of the stockholder's equity; though previously shown as a general residual equity, the amount of the dividend is converted by the formality of dividend declaration to a specific liability payable from current funds. As such, the dividend declaration reduces the current residual equity and is therefore reported in the fund statement. Under the cash approach to the fund statement such a transaction gives trouble; for, unless the dividend declaration is shown as an "application of funds," there is no hope of reconciling the fund statement with the balance sheet, except by a separate computation. Yet there still remains the vexing question, "What cash was involved in the declaration of the dividend?" By contrast, a dividend payable in stock would not appear in the fund statement under the fund theory. This, however, would not be because the dividend requires no cash disbursement but because the transaction did not affect the Current Fund. If the fund theory be applied specifically in these cases, the implied entries are, for the cash dividend:

Capital Fund:		
Earned surplus	$5,000	
Net working capital		$5,000
Current Fund:		
Current residual equity	5,000	
Dividend payable		5,000

whereas the stock dividend would require entry only in the Capital Fund:

Earned surplus	$8,000	
Surplus appropriated for stock dividend		$8,000

The acquisition or retirement of fixed assets, and their effects in the fund statement are more clearly related under the fund-theory approach. For example, a machine with a cost of $3,000, and an allowance for depreciation accumulated to the amount of $2,000 is traded in on a new machine for $1,000 against an agreed gross cost of $5,000, the difference of $4,000 being covered by the execution of instalment notes maturing within one year. The entries which presumably would be made in the two funds are:[31]

Current Fund:		
Transfer to Capital Fund for new machinery	$4,000	
Instalment notes payable		$4,000
Capital Fund:		
Machinery	5,000	
Allowance for depreciation of machinery	2,000	
Machinery		3,000
Net working capital		4,000

"Transfer to Capital Fund for new machinery" would be closed to current residual equity account, and the item would appear in the fund statement, despite the fact that no money was involved in the transaction. The trade-in aspects of the transaction would be entirely reported within the Capital Fund and would not affect the Current Fund at all; hence it would not appear in the fund statement.

A third way in which the fund theory (as applied through the double-fund notion of the balance sheet) is advantageous in the preparation of the fund statement has to do with those conversions or adjustments that seem to be inevitable, when income statement data are brought into the fund statement. The most common examples of this are depreciation, depletion, or other amortizations of fixed asset cost charged against current revenue. Much "educational" effort has been expended by accountants in the last hundred years to bring businessmen, lawyers, and others to a realization that these items are proper charges against current operations. How much that case is weakened by showing these charges added back in the fund statement—because they are "noncash" charges, or do not "require funds"—is only a matter of conjecture; but it would appear to be more than merely significant. To "add back" depreciation to the reported "net income" implies that, after all, depreciation is not a "real" cost; it is made to appear as an item that "does not have to be paid for," or merely a bookkeeping entry (i.e., one of those things which accountants do to "complicate" things). This kind of reaction leads to the conclusion that depreciation is a "take-it-or-leave-it" phenomenon. Not only does the awkwardness of the depreciation adjustment as shown in the fund statement undermine confidence in accounting reports—the adjustment of a figure that has been seriously and formally presented as the net and final "result" of operations can hardly be considered as anything but an undermining influence—but the ideas engendered by this procedure are dangerously misleading. Sound presentation should follow conventional cost allocations to the extent of recognizing the transfer of fixed asset cost to current operations, in terms of the entries that might be made in a funded system of accounts:

Capital Fund:		
Net working capital . .	$30,000	
Allowance for depreciation		$30,000
Current Fund:		
Inventory of goods in process	30,000	
Current residual equity . . .		30,000

The depreciation charge is, of course, absorbed at some time in the current "expense" along with other factory, selling, or administrative costs, and the income statement reports the absorption of this and other costs of factory operations to the extent that the goods are completed and sold. Hence, it may actually be incorrect to say that the depreciation charges are "added back" to the net income; the amount charged as depreciation is seldom absorbed completely in expense for the manufacturing situation and in the year in which it was charged. A more accurate description of the depreciation item in the fund statement would be:

Transfer from Capital Fund of fixed assets cost, reflected in current operations and inventories as depreciation	$30,000

This would not be a correction of the net income figure but would be reported as an item which increased the current residual equity by the amount of the depreciation charge, as a transfer from fixed capital.[32]

What has been said about depreciation applies with equal force to a number of other items. Certain situations tend to make these adjustments even more confusing than has been indicated. The use of the "combined statement of income and surplus" contributes to this. For instance, suppose that an outstanding issue of bonds has been retired by the exercise of a call privilege. The call premium, under extant usage, would appear as a charge in the combined statement of income and surplus. If the final figure (or any figure shown in the statement after this charge is deducted) is carried over into the statement of funds, a dilemma appears: either the expenditure for retiring the bonds must be shown exclusive of the call premium (which is not acceptable to a "cash" theory of the fund statement at all) or the same item must appear on both sections of the conventional fund statement, viz:[33]

Funds provided:	
By transactions during the year reported in the statement of income and surplus	$650,000
Add: Depreciation charges	30,000
Premium on bonds retired	10,000
Funds provided from operations	$690,000
Funds applied:	
To retirement of bonds (including the call premium of $10,000) . .	$510,000
To other items, including change in net working capital	180,000
Funds applied	$690,000

The addition of the call premium to "Funds provided from operations" cannot be defended on the grounds of being a "noncash charge"; it is added back for the sole reason that it should not (for the present purpose) have been shown in the income and surplus statement at all. The real situation is made clearer by reviewing the entries that would be made in a funded system of accounts:

	Debit	Credit
(1) Capital Fund:		
Call premium on bonds retired	$ 10,000	
Bonds payable	500,000	
Agreed liability for bond retirement		$510,000
(2) Current Fund:		
Transfer to Capital Fund for retirement of bonds (current residual equity)	510,000	
Cash in bank		510,000
(3) Capital Fund:		
Cash for retirement of bonds	510,000	
Net working capital		510,000
(4) Capital Fund:		
Agreed liability for bond retirement	510,000	
Cash for retirement of bonds		510,000

In this set of entries the retirement is considered a Capital Fund transaction in its entirety, except for the withdrawal of $510,000 of current funds for the indicated disbursement. The withdrawal of this amount from current operations is all that would need to appear in the fund statement if the call premium were not carried through the combined statement of income and surplus. Of course, the whole situation may be avoided if the figure taken from the combined statement of income and surplus to represent the "operating" effect upon funds is one "before other deductions and credits." Such a course, however, would seem to negate the "continuity" that is supposed to be espoused in the adoption of the "combined statement." Certainly it would still be somewhat puzzling to the reader. Further, it is not always practicable to seize upon such a figure, in view of the variety of items that may be reported together in the "capital costs" or "other charges and credits" section of the combined statement.

Then, too, it should be recognized that there is always the possibility of "credit adjustments"—deductions from, rather than additions to, the income figure taken from the "operating" report. A discount on bond retirement would require a credit adjustment of this kind. Now, since "adding back" is likely to be a universal necessity (in view of the ubiquitous depreciation, depletion, and amortization charges), the presence of both additions to and subtractions from the "operating" figure increases the feeling that accountants do not present things as simply and directly as they might; the reader may have an even more pronounced feeling that "income is not what it seems to be." Of course, this conclusion is unquestionably correct, for "income" is precisely that kind of a concept; this we pointed out earlier in the discussion. Yet the reader is bound to be disturbed when the "simple" concept of income is found to be so complex.

In this, as in other situations of financial accounting, there are two alternatives; one is to "educate the public," as the Institute Subcommittee on the Income Statement recommends. This, however, is not an easy task; it is nothing short of amazing to observe how slowly new ideas are assimilated even by young and curious minds in educational institutions under the pressure of formal educational processes. To educate the mass of laymen who have reason to read and use financial statements is nothing short of an Augean task. The easier alternative is for the accountant to recast his forms of reports so that the financial statements will say just what they are meant to say and so that their specific purposes are clearly defined. The present title of the fund statement is ambiguous and uninformative. It should be stated in terms that suggest the purpose and content of the report; perhaps (as a suggestion) it might be called "Summary of Transactions Affecting the Net Working Capital Position"; but, at all events, it should make no reference to funds, unless funds are the substance with which it deals. As we shall see, the fund theory would make another use of a variant of the present fund statement; under this usage it would have another function and another name.

A second way in which the statement might be made to fit its purpose a bit more closely, and a means of avoiding some of the confusion engendered by present practice, is to recast the content and arrangement of the data within the statement. The fund statement should be related to other reports for the same period, but it should stand on its own feet; it should not sprout from the shoulders of some other report. Paton presents a notable attempt in this direction:

M COMPANY

Statement of Funds, Year Ended December 31, 19——

Net sales and other earnings (1)		xxx
Current outlays for expenses, interest (2), and other deductions (3)		xxx
Earnings available before dividends		xxx
Disposition of capital assets (4)	xxx	
Less: Nonliquid receivables or property accepted (5)	xxx	xxx
Reduction of net working capital (see schedule)		xxx
Funds available from operations and conversions		xxx
Dividend appropriations		xxx
Balance of funds from operations and conversions		xxx
Long-term obligations issued during the year—net proceeds (6) less amount used or deposited to pay or retire long-term debt		xxx
Capital stock issued during the year—net proceeds (7) less cost of stock acquired or redeemed (8)		xxx
Funds acquired by bequest or gift	xxx	
Less: Amount of funds utilized for gifts and donations	xxx	xxx
Funds available for expansion and investment		xxx
Cost of plant additions and improvements	xxx	
Increase in investment in securities of affiliates	xxx	xxx
Balance of funds—increase in net working capital (see schedule)		xxx

(1) Net sales and all ancillary and special incomes and gains as shown by income sheet exclusive of the amount of **xxx**, profit on sale of capital assets, which is reported under another heading.

(2) Not including accumulation of bond discount shown under interest charges in income sheet in the amount of xxx, as such accumulation is reflected in a fixed liability.
(3) All expenses and deductions appearing in accompanying income statement, other than dividends, exclusive of charges not involving current outlays as follows: depreciation, xxx; amortization of patents, xxx.
(4) Charges connected with these transactions, except where included under "current outlays" above, have been deducted.
(5) In the sale of real estate a mortgage was taken in the amount of xxx.
(6) Par of debenture bonds issued, xxx; gross proceeds, xxx; commissions and other charges, xxx.
(7) Commissions and other costs attaching to this issue, xxx, are excluded.
(8) xxx shares of preferred stock acquired by call or market purchase during year at average cost of xxx per share.[34]

To be sure, this form of the fund statement is not without limitations. The use of specific subtotals and the extended footnotes could both be the basis for extensive discussion. The reference to "current outlays" for expenses, interest, taxes, and other deductions (and the footnote references to expense and interest items) make the interpretation of depreciation, amortization of patents, and the "accumulation of bond discount reflected in a fixed liability" rather difficult, especially since accountants maintain that depreciation and amortization are real costs which rank abreast with current outlays for expense[35] and that discount on a long-term obligation is a determinant of the true or effective rate of interest. But, regardless of these and other objections that might be raised,[36] the statement presented above does have the distinct merit of being reared on its own foundations and telling its own story (cross-referenced, if you please, to the income statement; but not sprouting from it). But even this statement shows the definite influence of traditional emphasis upon the income statement, and it also reflects the pattern of thought advanced in proprietary and entity theories; the statement as presented does not fit into the fund theory of accounting.

The fund statement, however, is useful as a first step in the process of developing a form of operating report that does meet the terms of the fund theory. It is possible to show in a single operating report not only all the data customarily shown in the typical income statement (without attempting to show any one explicitly computed income figure) but also all the information usually embraced by the statement of funds. Further, it is possible to show in such an operating report the effects of certain kinds of transactions which do not appear in conventional forms of financial reports except as footnotes or comments; this class of data may be shown completely without implication or prejudice toward any particular form or character of income statement or income computation. The relevant information may be taken from such a statement to construct any type of special purpose income figure that is desired, depending upon the needs and the purpose of the reader in making such abstracts. This form of statement is an accounting report rather than an interpretation, and it may be made as full and complete as may be desired.

The fund-theory operating report evolves naturally from what has already been said about the statement of funds. The statement of funds conventionally does include (by implication at least) all the force and effect of the income computation; hence it is easy to see how the income-statement data may be brought within the scope of an operating statement that is to express the operations under the fund-theory approach. However, the conventional statement of funds is set up from but a single viewpoint—that of the current fund—as has been explained. It is first necessary to reframe the statement of funds so as to recognize the specific fund units.

For the present purpose we have taken the distinction between current assets and equities and those considered as "noncurrent" as the basis for fund units. The preceding chapter described a form of balance sheet for the current and the capital funds based upon these distinctions. Of course, it is possible to establish separate funds on other bases. It might, for instance, be desirable to separate investment operations from both current and capital funds and to establish a separate investment fund for accounting purposes that would parallel the administrative, functional, or other lines of cleavage that mark out investment operations as separate from the others. Or there might be other classifications along similar lines. It is possible to view even the current assets and equities as separable into two classes: "financial" and "operating" assets. The significance of cash and receivables is largely that of dollar claims; some of the "current" liabilities are also of this nature—purely dollar claims and obligations. On the other hand, the inventories and prepayments are distinctly different from dollar claims, even though deferred costs may fit conventional notions of "currentness." Trade payables arise largely from those operations that are related to inventory and operations and are thus perhaps to be distinguished from pure dollar advances. Thus there might be established two separate "current" funds, one to cover purely financing transactions, the other to encompass the operating aspects of short-term commitments in assets, equities, revenue, and expense. But the balance sheet is not the only basis for establishing fund units; it is possible to recognize in establishing funds for accounting purposes the major aspects of internal organization or the segregation of lines of product, territorial differentiations, and the like. A company that engages in several lines of activity that are widely differentiated will nearly always separate the accounting classifications for each of these activities for internal control purposes; it is equally possible to report over-all financial effects in terms of such fund units. For example, a financial report might show separately such activities as maintaining and operating an office building; carrying on mining, transportation, steelmaking, or cement production; promulgating research on products, methods, and other phases of technology; or any one of a host of other operations usually recognized in the separate incorporation of "subsidiaries," such as insurance, shipbuilding, special government contracts, or any one of a large number of widespread activities. Thus, there might be reflected in separate fund reports as much detail with respect to each of these operations as might be desired. This is already recognized in practice, when the reports of subsidiary companies are included with the over-all financial reports of the affiliated group; the point to be made here is that separate incorporation is not necessary to establish specific fund units. One of the major weaknesses of the "consolidated" report is that a good many things are there combined which are in essence separate; this weakness may be just as real when the fund units are not separately incorporated and are therefore ignored. The legal fiction of corporate entity is no insurance against the conglomeration of many different activities under the heading of a single set of reports.

Still, to the extent that there are advantages in "consolidating" all the various activities into financial summaries of broad scope, there is nothing to prevent the consolidation of any and all information that is available, since the "fund lines" may be erased as easily as they are drawn in the first place, so long as the new fund concept is properly applied, as was indicated in chapter iv. The fund notion is flexible enough to be applied to new situations and to be developed in such fashion as will best meet the needs and conditions which will arise from time to time.

For the present purpose, however, it will suffice to consider only the current-capital segregation of funds. This serves to illustrate the principles that are involved; it is based upon criteria of fund separation that—however difficult they may be to apply to a particular item in a specific context—are generally recognized and employed in practice, as important distinctions to be maintained in financial reporting. To illustrate, consider the following case:[37]

WYMAN COMPANY

CONDENSED BALANCE-SHEET DATA AS OF DECEMBER 31, 1939

	1938	1939
Cash	$ 122,000	$ 93,000
Marketable securities	. . . .	65,000
Receivables	293,000	294,000
Inventories	860,000	888,000
Prepayments	26,000	28,000
Real estate bonds	55,000	25,000
Investment in Hart Company stock	. . . .	640,000
Land	734,000	884,000
Buildings and equipment	2,180,000	2,120,000
Good-will	25,000	25,000
Bond discount	. . . .	5,000
Organization costs	5,000	10,000
Total debits	$4,300,000	$5,077,000
Current liabilities	$ 490,000	$ 511,000
First-mortgage bonds outstanding	15,000	350,000
Reserve for depreciation	713,000	883,000
Reserve for uncollectibles	25,000	30,000
Capital stock, preferred	200,000	
Capital stock, common	300,000	525,000
Donated surplus	252,000	402,000
Earned surplus	930,000	1,046,000
Appreciation surplus	1,375,000	1,330,000
Total credits	$4,300,000	$5,077,000

WYMAN COMPANY

CONDENSED INCOME SHEET AND SURPLUS DATA
YEAR ENDED DECEMBER 31, 1939

Net sales	$2,400,000
Cost of sales, including depreciation	2,345,000
Interest and rentals earned	7,000
Dividends received on Hart Company stock	52,000
Taxes (assumed to be federal income taxes)	13,000
Interest charges	15,000
Premium paid on retirement of preferred stock	1,000
Dividends paid on preferred stock	14,000
Realized appreciation	45,000

SUPPLEMENTARY INFORMATION

(1) All assets are reported on a cost basis, subject to accrued depreciation and estimated uncollectibles, except land, buildings and equipment, and good-will.
(2) Real estate bonds were collected in cash during the year in the amount of $30,000.
(3) Additions to buildings and equipment during the year, at cost, amount to $10,000.
(4) Par was received for all mortgage bonds issued during the year, except a block amounting to $100,000 par, which was sold on December 31, 1939.
(5) The increase in organization costs represents actual outlays made in connection with issue of securities during the year.
(6) Charges to depreciation reserve during the year, arising in connection with sales and retirements of equipment, total $30,000; credits amount to $200,000.
(7) The increase in donated surplus during 1939 results from receipt of property as a gift to the Company.
(8) Cost of Sales includes a net "loss on retirement" from retirement and sale of equipment, as of January 1, 1939. $35,000; the proceeds of this sale in cash totaled $5,000.

The financial reports that would be used to summarize the data given, under conventional methods and forms of reporting, are presented below:

WYMAN COMPANY

STATEMENT OF INCOME AND SURPLUS
YEAR ENDED DECEMBER 31, 1945

Net sales		$2,400,000
Cost of sales (including depreciation of $200,000 of which $45,000 is depreciation on the appraisal increment)		2,310,000
Operating net revenue		90,000
Other income:		
Interest and rentals earned	$ 7,000	
Dividends on Hart Company stock	52,000	59,000
Total net income		149,000
Deduct interest charges		15,000
Net income before taxes		134,000
Deduct taxes on income		13,000
Net profit to stockholders		121,000
Deduct preferred-stock dividends		14,000
Net profit to common stockholders		107,000
Earned surplus balance, January 1, 1939		930,000
Addition to surplus from realized appreciation		45,000
Deduction from surplus for		
Loss on sale of fixed assets	35,000	
Premium on preferred-stock retired	1,000	36,000*
Earned surplus, per balance sheet, 12/31/39		$1,046,000

* Indicates decrease.

WYMAN COMPANY

Fund Statement, Year Ended December 31, 1939

Funds provided:		
Net profit to stockholders, per combined statement of income and surplus	$121,000	
Add: Depreciation charges	200,000	
Funds provided from operations		$321,000
Realization of real estate bonds		30,000
Sales of equipment—net proceeds		5,000
Issuance of new bonds payable—net proceeds		330,000
Issuance of new common stock—net proceeds		225,000
Total funds provided		$911,000
Funds applied:		
Dividends on preferred stock	14,000	
Acquisition of Hart Company stock	640,000	
Additions to buildings and equipment	10,000	
Retirement of preferred stock	201,000	
Outlays for fees, commissions, etc.	5,000	
Increase in net working capital, per schedule	41,000	
Total funds applied	$911,000	

COMPARATIVE SCHEDULE OF WORKING CAPITAL

Current assets:			
Increased marketable securities	$65,000		
Increased inventories	28,000		
Increased prepayments	2,000	$ 95,000	
Less: Decreased receivables	4,000		
Decreased cash	29,000	33,000	$ 62,000
Current liability increase			21,000
Increase in net working capital			$ 41,000

Recasting the same data into statements based upon the fund approach, the balance sheet is presented in double-account form, with the exception that the balance of the current residual equity is not carried into the capital balance sheet. Thus, there are separated the two elements of surplus or residual equity: (1) the current fund portion and (2) the long-term or capital portion. There are advantages in the separation of these two surplus elements. It makes a substantial difference whether the assets restricted by the residual equity are current or of long-term character, and the separation of the surplus equity into these two elements makes this distinction. Further, by this process, attention is called to the important financial operation of transferring funds from current to long-term activities, or vice versa.

WYMAN COMPANY

Balance Sheet—Current Fund, Years Ended December 31

Assets	1938	1939	Increase
Cash	$ 122,000	$ 93,000	$ 29,000*
Receivables (net book value)	268,000	264,000	4,000*
Inventories	860,000	888,000	28,000
Prepayments	26,000	28,000	2,000
Total current assets	$1,276,000	$1,273,000	$ 3,000*
Equities			
Current liabilities	$ 490,000	$ 511,000	$ 21,000
Current residual equity	786,000	762,000	24,000*
Total current equities	$1,276,000	$1,273,000	$ 3,000*

WYMAN COMPANY

Balance Sheet—Capital Fund, Years Ended December 31

Assets	1938	1939	Increase
Marketable securities	....	$ 65,000	$ 65,000
Real estate bonds	$ 55,000	25,000	30,000*
Investment in Hart Company stock	....	640,000	640,000
Land	734,000	884,000	150,000
Buildings and equipment (net)	1,467,000	1,237,000	230,000*
Good-will	25,000	25,000	....
Organization costs	5,000	10,000	5,000
Total capital assets	$2,286,000	$2,886,000	$600,000
Equities			
Bonded debt (less discount)	$ 15,000	$ 345,000	$330,000
Capital stock—preferred	200,000	....	200,000*
Capital stock—common	300,000	525,000	225,000
Donated surplus	252,000	402,000	150,000
Appreciation reserve	1,375,000	1,330,000	45,000*
Capital Fund residual equity	144,000	284,000	140,000
Total capital equities	$2,286,000	$2,886,000	$600,000

* Indicates decrease.

Two significant points should be noted in this statement. First, marketable securities are listed in the Capital Fund, on the ground that the Current Fund covers the main line of operations and that an investment in marketable securities is in fact a withdrawal of funds from the current operations. The other point is that the separation of the two elements of the general surplus reveals a definite transfer of working assets to capital uses; this "freezing" of current resources is important and should be shown; the funded balance sheet reveals it at a glance by the comparison of the changes in these two very different kinds of "surplus."

The operating reports prepared to accompany these fund balance sheets are "tied in" to the changes in the current and the capital surplus equities; they are in fact summaries of the transactions behind those changes. These statements are presented below:

WYMAN COMPANY

OPERATING REPORT, CURRENT FUND, YEAR ENDED DECEMBER 31, 1939

Additions to current residual equity:		
Net sales revenue	$2,400,000	
Dividends, Hart Company	52,000	
Interest and rentals earned	7,000	
Fixed asset charges transferred from capital for absorption in current operations (per Capital Fund Report)	200,000	
Gross additions to current residual equity		$2,659,000
Deductions from current residual equity:		
Cost of sales, excluding depreciation or losses on property retirements	2,110,000	
Depreciation	200,000	
Taxes	13,000	
Interest	15,000	
Dividends on preferred stock	14,000	
Total deductions from current residual equity		2,352,000
Balance available for expansion or conversion		307,000
Less: Transfers to capital account		331,000
Net decrease in current residual equity		$ 24,000

WYMAN COMPANY

OPERATING REPORT, CAPITAL FUND, YEAR ENDED DECEMBER 31, 1939

Capital expenditures:		
Land, acquired by donation	$150,000	
Purchase of Hart Company stock	640,000	
Addition to buildings and equipment	10,000	
Retirement of preferred stock	201,000	
Outlays for fees, commissions, etc.	5,000	
Purchase of marketable securities	65,000	$1,071,000
Financed by:		
Gift of donated land	150,000	
Issuance of bonds (net proceeds)	330,000	
Realization of real estate bonds	30,000	
Issuance of common stock	225,000	
Proceeds of fixed-asset retirements	5,000	740,000
Funds supplied from current operations		331,000
Equity deductions:		
Fixed asset charges absorbed in current operations (per current fund report)	200,000	
Less: Amortization of appraisal increment	45,000	
Net fixed asset cost absorption	155,000	
Premium on retirement of preferred stock	1,000	
Underdepreciation of fixed assets retired	35,000	191,000
Net increase in residual equity, capital fund		$ 140,000

It should be noted that the operating statements reflect every bit of information that is customarily shown in *both* the income statement and the fund statement and that each of these statements presents a detailed account of the net residual equity change in the accompanying fund balance sheet. Of course, neither of the statements shows the "income" of the period; this is in keeping with the position developed in the exposition of chapter iii. The income figure, as was pointed out, is one which has different significance for different purposes, and there is no one concept of income that fits all these purposes. Yet, if the reader of these statements wants to establish an income computation, all the available data are presented, and he may arrange them as may suit his situation. Statements of this character tend to focus attention upon the details of operation and the transactions which have occurred and to call forth the kind of analysis that should precede any attempt to evaluate the income of a given period. The sum of the residual equity changes in both funds is precisely the same as that which would appear in conventional analysis of surplus or in the combined statement of income and surplus.

One interesting question arises in these statements with respect to the handling of depreciation charges. These appear both as additions to the Current Fund and as deductions in the same statement. Although at first glance this seems a bit awkward, it is really an accurate statement of the case. The depreciation charge is, after all, a transfer of fixed-asset cost[38] to current operations, and the absorption of this charge is an essential element of expense. The transfer appears in both the Capital and the Current funds, since both are affected; the absorption, however, is a Current Fund item. Actually, there should be some difference between the transferred amount and that absorbed, because of the variation in inventory with respect to depreciation charges there impounded. This has been ignored in this case, both in the orthodox and in the "funded" statements. For reasons already given, this difference would be small in most situations; but it could be recognized if the inventory costs were analyzed to separate depreciation, depletion, and amortization from other types of cost.

One other point arises in the presentation that has been attempted; this has to do with the handling of the donation of land. Orthodox methods of reporting would limit this transaction to a mere balance-sheet change that would be ignored in the operating reports (income statement and statement of funds); unless there were presented an analysis of donated surplus account, the reader would be left to interpret this change by inference. However, this transaction is of sufficient significance to merit better treatment; it is therefore reported in the operating statement of the Capital Fund, in preference to allowing it to be completely unexplained, or but mentioned in a footnote to accompany the financial statements.

The operating reports as thus presented follow the major tenets of the fund theory; these notions are summarized here, to clarify and emphasize the position from which they are developed:

1. Under the fund theory, accounting is viewed as one of the specialized branches of quantitative method—a special form of statistical procedure. From this position, accounting is concerned with the quantification of certain business facts in financial terms and the reporting of these quantified data in some systematic and summary fashion, without reference to the persons into whose hands the reports may come, or to the purposes for which they may be used; rather, it is admitted that facts may have different significance to different persons and that it is impossible to meet every need in a set of financial reports, although it is possible to present sufficient details to permit the use of the reports in such a way as the readers may require. Accounting does not deal with persons and personal rights, except as these relate to the statistical nature of the situation and the data.

2. Valuation, as such, is not exclusively an accounting matter, although value notions and their derivatives are used in accounting processes. Thus, the fund theory does not of itself "take a position" with respect to the methods of valuation but views such methods as means of quantifying the data with which accounting must deal. The basis of cost has importance in its relation to the historical phase of financial reporting, but other bases may have application when important financial facts can be presented fairly only by the recognition of valuation bases that have sufficient objectivity (in the sense of social consensus) to convey meaning to the reader.

3. The central concept in the fund theory is that of an area of operations, a center of interest, or the scope of attention to be encompassed by the accounting process and financial reports. The criteria that serve to define a fund are often arbitrary, but they relate generally to specified purposes, activities, situations, or modes of procedure—frequently, these are themselves integrated with some phases of managerial organization and control. The fund is not coexistent with any legal or physical person; its principal attribute of tangibility is the collection of assets within it. However, both legal and actual persons may be related to funds in a number of ways: e.g., managers, legal claimants, equitable beneficiaries, sponsors, or the members of organizations that stand in such capacities.

4. As is the case with all patterns of theory, the significance of the fund theory evolves from those operational concepts that are related to, and give expression to, the central

notion. There are four such operational concepts in the fund theory:

a) *Assets*.—These are neither physical things nor financial phenomena but economic service potentials. They draw their existence and their meaning from the nature and the scope of operations of the fund.

b) *Equities*.—As distinct from the notions of obligation or legal liability, equities are restrictions upon, or reservations that apply to the assets of the fund; they may arise from legal, equitable, economic, or even managerial considerations. Although some equities are removed by the process of disbursement, they may be discharged or they may disappear for a considerable number of reasons. Their relations to assets are usually indirect; rarely is there a specific pattern of relationship between assets and equities, except that the total of equities must be equal to the total of assets, because of the residual restriction embodied in the definition of the fund itself.

c) *Revenue*.—The appearance of new assets within a fund unaccompanied by any specific equity restriction is revenue; or, assets that appear with restrictions may be the basis for revenue when those restrictions are removed. Of course, residual equity applies to all assets; the essence of revenue lies in the absence of specific restrictions, not in the notion of residual claims.

d) *Expense*.—The outward flow of services from the fund to various interested or noninterested parties represents the accomplishment of the purposes for which the operations are carried on. In this connection, distinction must be maintained between the purpose of the fund and the purposes of investment; if this distinction is maintained, there is no difficulty involved in defining expense in terms of accomplishment of that purpose to which the fund is dedicated. Expense may take the form of tangible goods, services in the ordinary sense, or mere benefits transferred in some measurable form as a result of fund operation; it is the economic, not the physical, attributes that distinguish assets and expense from other things. In its simplest form, expense is the release of assets from the fund toward the accomplishment of the objectives of the fund.

5. The fund theory does not embrace a concept of income, for the reason that income is not definable unless it includes a recognition of the situation and the purposes that relate to it. Further, the separation of the fund from the persons (legal or actual) who may have interests in the results of fund activities makes "income" a relatively meaningless term; income must be related to an economic subject to have any real significance, and that significance depends upon the subject to a large extent.

6. The definition of a fund is flexible (as opposed to the definitions of "proprietor" or "corporate entity"); therefore, the operating reports and balance sheets may be established to recognize any desired division of subject matter or any combination of activities that is of sufficient importance to merit special treatment. There may also be any desired degree of "consolidation" of fund reports so as to bring together for some purposes details which for other purposes should be kept in separate categories. Hence, departmental, territorial, or commodity areas may be defined for certain purposes and reported upon without reference to personal or legal relationships. Similarly, any number of corporate or other forms of enterprises that are established as separate funds for some purposes may be combined (with appropriate adjustments) into larger funds to meet other purposes.

The materials presented in this chapter have served to develop some of the uses of fund theory in presenting the results of operations in financial reports. A more comprehensive application of the principles that have been discussed is made in an extended hypothetical illustration which is presented in the following chapter.

CHAPTER VII

FUND PRINCIPLES APPLIED TO THE FORM OF FINANCIAL REPORTS

THE discussion and argument of the preceding chapters have served to establish the general viewpoint and the basic principles of fund theory; in this presentation there have also appeared some general ideas as to the mode of reporting which might be employed, in keeping with the theoretical structure that has been proposed. To make more clear the implications of the fund theory, and to point out the various possibilities in reporting on a fund basis, this chapter is devoted to the presentation of a fairly comprehensive illustration of fund-reporting as applied to an industrial corporation.

The materials used in the illustration are really adapted from the published reports of an actual corporation; but to maintain simplicity in dealing with the figures, and to bring out in detail the possibilities offered by a fund basis of financial reporting, two changes have been made in the original data. First, the original figures have been "rounded off" to reduce their arithmetic complexity and make them easier to follow; second, some purely hypothetical material has been added for the purpose of exhibiting certain effects in the statements. Because of these alterations, the illustration is referred to as a hypothetical case; and we shall refer to the corporation involved in this case as "Mythical Corporation."

As an approach to the discussion and development of this illustration, the following financial statements are presented in conventional form, as they might appear in an ordinary annual report:

MYTHICAL CORPORATION

Comparative Balance Sheets, as at December 31, 19X1 and 19X2

ASSETS	19X1	19X2	Increase
Current assets:			
Cash on hand and in banks	$ 942,000	$ 1,412,000	$ 470,000
Notes and accounts receivable	1,762,000	2,295,000	533,000
Inventories (at cost)	3,548,000	4,070,000	522,000
Interest and dividends receivable	6,000	4,000	2,000*
Prepayments	8,000	14,000	6,000
Total current assets	$ 6,266,000	$ 7,795,000	$1,529,000
Investments:			
Bonds of other companies (at cost)	$ 185,000	$ 160,000	$ 25,000*
Stocks of other companies (at cost)	248,000	240,000	8,000*
Investment in subsidiary (at cost)	378,000	378,000	....
Loan to subsidiary company	....	40,000	40,000
Sinking fund, bonds payable	81,450	166,670	85,220
Total investments	$ 892,450	$ 894,670	$ 92,220
Fixed assets:			
Plant, machinery, and equipment—Gross cost	$ 4,488,000	$ 4,782,000	$ 294,000
Less allowance for depreciation	1,124,000	1,231,000	107,000
Net total fixed assets	$ 3,364,000	$ 3,551,000	$ 187,000
Total assets	$10,522,450	$12,330,670	$1,808,220
EQUITIES			
Current liabilities:			
Trade accounts payable	$ 1,100,000	$ 1,530,000	$ 430,000
Bank loans	....	500,000	500,000
Accrued wages and interest payable	199,000	408,875	209,875
Local, state, and federal taxes	1,218,000	1,072,000	146,000*
Total current liabilities	$ 2,517,000	$ 3,510,875	$ 993,875
Funded debt:			
First mortgage 5 per cent sinking-fund bonds	$ 1,000,000	$ 1,000,000	....
Stockholders' interests:			
Preferred stock, $8, nonparticipating	$ 1,300,000	....	$1,300,000*
Common stock, no par value	1,200,000	$ 2,710,000	1,510,000
Reserves: Additional war costs	....	200,000	200,000
Maintenance and repairs	280,000	328,000	48,000
Unrestricted earned surplus	4,225,450	4,581,795	356,345
Total stockholders' interests	$ 7,005,450	$ 7,819,795	$ 814,345
Total equities	$10,522,450	$12,330,670	$1,808,220

* Indicates decrease.

MYTHICAL CORPORATION

Statement of Income and Earned Suprlus, Year Ended December 31, 19X2

Net sales			$24,595,000
Expense:			
Materials, supplies, and miscellaneous		$15,183,000	
Wages and other employment costs		6,781,000	
State and local taxes		369,000	
Depreciation and amortization		418,000	
Repair and maintenance charges		141,000	
Total costs incurred		22,892,000	
Less: Increase in inventory		522,000	
Operating expense			22,370,000
Net income from operations			2,225,000
Interest and dividend income			15,000
Gross income, before net charges and distributions			2,240,000
Nonoperating deductions:			
Interest charges on bonds and notes payable		57,875	
Sinking-fund trustee's fee		1,000	
Provision for additional war costs		200,000	
Charges, retirement of preferred stock		53,000	
Total		311,875	
Less:			
Gain on sale of investments	$5,000		
Adjustment, allowance for uncollectibles, prior year	3,000		
Gain on sale of fixed assets	6,000		
Discount on reacquired bonds	2,220	16,220	
Net charges against income			295,655
Net income, before federal taxes			1,944,345
Federal taxes on income			1,062,000
Net income for the year, to surplus			882,345
Add: Surplus balance, January 1, 19X2			4,225,450
Total			5,107,795
Deduct:			
Cash dividends on preferred stock		104,000	
Cash dividends on common stock		272,000	
Share dividends on common stock		150,000	526,000
Surplus balance, at December 31, 19X2			$ 4,581,795

MYTHICAL CORPORATION

STATEMENT OF APPLICATION OF FUNDS, YEAR ENDED DECEMBER 31, 19X2

Funds provided:		
From operations:		
Gross income, before charges and federal tax per statement of income and earned surplus		$2,240,000
Add: Depreciation and amortization	$418,000	
Repairs and maintenance	141,000	
Charges to operations not requiring funds		559,000
Funds provided by operations		2,799,000
Proceeds from retirement of fixed assets		27,000
Proceeds from sale of stocks	50,000	
Proceeds from sale of bonds	20,000	
Funds from sales of investments		70,000
Proceeds from additional common stock issued		1,360,000
Total funds provided		$4,256,000
Funds applied:		
Plant additions		$ 626,000
Retirement of preferred stock		1,353,000
Federal taxes on income		1,062,000
Contributions to bond sinking fund (including trustee's fee)		84,000
Interest charges		57,875
Repairs and maintenance expenditures		93,000
Investment in stocks of other companies		32,000
Loans to affiliated company		40,000
Cash dividends, preferred stock		104,000
Cash dividends, common stock		272,000
Net increase in net working capital	535,125	
Less: Adjustment for uncollectibles, prior year	3,000	532,125
Total funds applied		$4,256,000
Net working capital change:		
Increased current assets, per comparative balance sheets		$1,529,000
Less: Increased current liabilities		993,875
Net increase in net working capital		$ 535,125

Some comment on these financial statements seems indicated at the outset. No attempt has been made here to present anything but a reasonably close approximation to conventional forms of reports. There are items and modes of presentation in these statements to which some accountants might object; the arrangement of the statement of income and earned surplus is probably not one to which all practitioners would agree, and there might even be some disagreement as to the form and classification in the balance sheet. Moreover, the statement of funds is prepared on the premise that such statements have to do with "cash" transactions; as a result, a somewhat awkward reconciliation is required, to make the change in net working capital as shown in the balance sheet agree with the balancing item in the statement of funds.[1] The only other way to handle the adjustment to uncollectibles of the prior year (if the cash approach is to be followed) is to adjust the 19X1 balance sheet for this item. But these difficulties need not concern us greatly at this point, so long as the reader is aware that we are merely attempting to start with a reasonably well-stated set of financial reports, to serve as a backdrop against which to discuss this illustrative case.

It was pointed out in the preceding chapter that there is no reason why the operations of an industrial firm might not be divided into any desired number of funds. Although we there employed as criteria for the separation of funds the commonly accepted notions of current and fixed classifications on the balance sheet, it was pointed out that a number of other criteria might be employed and that the number of funds to be recognized in the accounting reports would depend upon just what degree of importance should be attached to various aspects of the situation. In the present case, we divide the activities into six fund units: Cash and Banks Fund, General Operating Fund, Investment Fund, Current Sinking Fund, Invested Sinking Fund, and Capital Fund.

Cash and Banks Fund.—This fund includes the operations of financing in general, and all cash receipts and disbursements are reported within this fund. Since the relation between bank loans, overdrafts, and demand deposits is so close, the fund is defined (from the point of view of the balance sheet) to include not only cash in bank and cash awaiting deposit but also the current or floating bank debt. Cash working funds are here included with other bank and cash items for the sake of simplicity, since departmental funds are not employed in this illustration. The comparative balance sheet for this fund would appear as follows:

MYTHICAL CORPORATION

CASH AND BANKS FUND

COMPARATIVE BALANCE SHEET, AS AT DECEMBER 31, 19X1 AND 19X2

ASSETS	19X1	19X2	Increase
Cash on hand and in banks	$942,000	$1,412,000	$470,000
EQUITIES			
Bank loans	....	$ 500,000	$500,000
Residual equity	$942,000	912,000	30,000*
Total equities	$942,000	$1,412,000	$470,000

* Indicates decrease.

The operating report for this fund would, in view of the nature of the assets and equities in the fund and the nature of the transactions which occur within it, be prepared on a "cash" basis of accounting, and the operating report would be substantially the same as the conventional statement of cash receipts and disbursements. The only exception to this arises from the fact that the bank loans are reported as an equity restriction as well as a source of cash. The operating report for this fund is shown below:

MYTHICAL CORPORATION

CASH AND BANKS FUND

REPORT OF OPERATIONS, YEAR ENDED DECEMBER 31, 19X2

Additions:		
From new bank loans		$ 500,000
From General Operating Fund:		
Collections from trade receivables		24,065,000
From Investment Fund:		
Proceeds from sales of securities	$ 70,000	
Interest and dividends collected	17,000	87,000
From Capital Fund:		
Additional common stock issued	1,360,000	
Sale of retired plant assets	27,000	1,387,000
Gross additions		26,039,000
Deductions:		
Settlement of floating debt, general operations:		
Materials, supplies, and miscellaneous costs	14,759,000	
Wages and interest	6,633,000	
State, local, and federal taxes	1,577,000	22,969,000
Cash dividends on preferred and common shares		376,000
Transfer to Investment Fund:		
Acquisition of new investment shares	32,000	
Loans made to subsidiary company	40,000	72,000
Transfer to Sinking Fund:		
Regular annual contribution		80,000
Transfer to Capital Fund:		
Additions to plant assets	626,000	
Retirement of preferred stock	1,353,000	
Repairs and maintenance expenditures	93,000	2,072,000
Total deductions		25,569,000
Balance, before restrictions		470,000
Less: Restriction for repayment of bank loans		500,000
Net decrease in fund equity		$ 30,000

General Operating Fund.—The activities covered by the accounts of this fund are those which make up the main line of manufacturing and sales. It would be possible, of course, to subdivide this fund to show separately the results of different classes of such operations, as might be indicated by commodity, territorial, or functional departmentation within the firm's organization; however, for the present purpose such breakdowns are not attempted. The data that are reported from the General Operating Fund are represented by those assets and equities ordinarily considered to fall within the "current" category, except for cash and bank accounts and those related to investment operations which are included in other funds; from the point of view of the operating report, the data for this fund include most of the items usually presented in the "operating" section of conventional income statements. In addition, however, certain other items of current significance—such as the accrual of interest costs, the declaration of dividends payable in cash, and the obligations for taxes (including federal income tax) are also reported in this fund. The comparative balance sheets and the operating report for the General Operating Fund are shown below:

MYTHICAL CORPORATION

GENERAL OPERATING FUND

COMPARATIVE BALANCE SHEETS, AS AT DECEMBER 31, 19X1 AND 19X2

	19X1	19X2	Increase
ASSETS			
Notes and accounts receivable	$1,762,000	$2,295,000	$533,000
Inventories (at cost)	3,548,000	4,070,000	522,000
Unrealized appreciation	157,000	....	157,000*
Unrealized declination	....	135,000*	135,000*
Prepayments	8,000	14,000	6,000
Total assets	$5,475,000	$6,244,000	$769,000
EQUITIES			
Payable, materials, supplies, and misc.	$1,100,000	$1,530,000	$430,000
Payable, for wages and interest	201,000	413,000	212,000
Payable, state and federal taxes	1,218,000	1,072,000	146,000*
Residual equity	2,956,000	3,229,000	273,000
Total equities	$5,475,000	$6,244,000	$769,000

* Indicates decrease or deduction.

MYTHICAL CORPORATION

GENERAL OPERATING FUND

REPORT OF OPERATIONS, YEAR ENDED DECEMBER 31, 19X2

Financing:			
Collection of trade receivables, per cash and Bank Fund report			$24,065,000
Less: Settlements of floating debt		$22,969,000	
Cash dividends paid		376,000	23,345,000
Net decrease in fund equity from financing transactions			720,000
Transfers, valuations, and adjustments:			
Additions to fund equity:			
Revenue from sales (net)		24,595,000	
Revaluation of receivables, prior year		3,000	
Depreciation and amortization, transferred from Capital Fund		418,000	
Provision for maintenance and repairs—			
Actual expenditures	$93,000		
Estimated undermaintenance	48,000	141,000	
Gross additions to fund equity		25,157,000	
Deductions from Fund Equity:			
Operating expense (Schedule A)		22,370,000	
Interest charges		64,000	
Dividends declared		376,000	
Inventory appreciation, prior year		157,000	
Inventory declination, current year		135,000	
Provision for federal income tax		1,062,000	
Gross deductions from fund equity		$24,164,000	
Net increase in fund equity, exclusive of financing			993,000
Net increase in fund equity			$ 273,000

SCHEDULE A

GENERAL OPERATING FUND

COMPUTATION OF EXPENSE, YEAR ENDED DECEMBER 31, 19X2

Costs:	
Inventory, carried over from 19X1	$ 3,548,000
Current charges:	
Materials, supplies, and miscellaneous	15,183,000
Wages and other employment costs	6,781,000
Sales and excise taxes assessed	143,000
Taxes on real and personal property	226,000
Depreciation and amortization	418,000
Estimated charge for repairs and maintenance	141,000
Gross cost of operations	26,440,000
Less: Inventory carried forward to 19X3	4,070,000
Operating expense	$22,370,000

In these reports for the General Operating Fund may be seen the way in which certain items of "unrealized gain or loss" may be reported. The inventories have been valued on both historical and current replacement cost bases, and contra or adjunct accounts are employed to show these alternative valuations in the balance sheets. The unrealized appreciation in the initial inventory of 19x2 has been clearly labeled as such in the comparative balance sheet, and its effect upon the fund equity is shown within the report of operations; similarly, the unrealized declination in the closing inventory appears in both reports. Since the reader has both these sets of data, he may employ them as may best suit his situation. If it is desirable to employ historical cost exclusively for the income computation, the reader may use those data; if an exclusively replacement cost basis is to be followed, the necessary information is at hand; and, if for some reason it is desired to use the notion of aggregate cost or aggregate market, whichever is the lower—the data for such a computation is available.[2]

The computation of expense is made entirely without reference to the unrealized appreciation or declination of inventory; the reader will recall that expense was defined in an earlier chapter as the current cost of services released from the firm to the market, as measured by the delivery of goods or the rendering of whatever perquisites make up the "product" of the operations. It should be noted also, in connection with the computation of expense, that this illustration does not consider the effects of alternative methods of establishing historical cost; that is, we have not specified whether the "cost" was determined by first-in-first-out, last-in-first-out, base-stock, weighted-moving-average, or other costing procedure. This is because—in the last analysis—these methods are but different approaches to the problem of joint cost involved in separating the aggregate acquisitions (which encompass varying prices, different quantities, and perhaps other unspecified variables) into two categories: (1) the stream of issues from stores that has been maintained during the period and (2) the retentions in stores held over to the following fiscal period as a future charge to expense. In the present state of our knowledge, every allocation of joint cost is colored with some degree of arbitrariness and expediency; this writer has no intention of entering this complex area for purposes of this illustration. But—and it should be noted carefully—if there are shown in the financial statements *both* the aggregate market replacement cost and the aggregate historical cost however determined, the major needs of the reader of financial statements will be better served than by any blind emphasis upon a single-phase "cost" figure. Indeed, showing both these valuations removes (in this writer's opinion) most of the arguments that have been waged over the effect of alternative methods of calculating "cost" by last-in-first-out as opposed to other inventory computations. The effects of different cost computations upon the amount of income taxes and their relation to price or output policy may be dismissed from the present discussion as irrelevant to the immediate purpose. Taxable income is quite obviously a highly technical concept; it is a variant of "income" that is defined within strict limits for one special purpose; since fund theory does not embrace any specific concept of income, tax procedures and their effects lie outside the field of present discussion. As to price policy, it should be apparent that prices are not set from income calculations, nor need they be based upon any specialized concept of cost as established by some method of historical allocation. To the extent that costs enter price policy at all, they must reflect current alternatives (in the form of choices between various methods of manufacture and shadings of quality in the finished product) in terms of current market prices rather than historical "facts." Further, it should never be forgotten that the purchaser plays an important role in the determination of prices, so long as any form of competition for his patronage exists.

It will be noted that depreciation and amortization appears in this illustration (just as it did in the preceding chapter) as a transfer from the Capital Fund to the General Operating Fund of long-term costs to be absorbed in current operations. The reasons for this treatment have already been presented; but the reader may object to the similar treatment accorded maintenance and repair charges, especially since these are only in part current expenditures. It may seem difficult to justify the amount of estimated undermaintenance as a transfer from the Capital Fund, since there is no legal liability involved, and no "apparent" cost incurred. There are, however, two things to be considered before this treatment is dismissed as undesirable. In the first place, the depreciation and amortization charges are actually based upon some policy of maintenance and repair. The concept of use-life upon which such charges are based is meaningless unless some assumption is made as to the maintenance and repair policy, for any asset may be used long past its normal period of usefulness if the mounting costs of maintenance will be met. The real reason for the retirement of long-term assets lies in most cases in the outlook for additional costs to be suffered by continuing the period of service, as opposed to other available alternatives; repairs and maintenance charges are thus an important element in the use-life of long-term assets and the resulting depreciation or amortization charges. But, in addition to the fact that depreciation and maintenance policies are thus so closely intertwined, there is another reason for the treatment that has been accorded the maintenance and repair charges in this illustration. This is that, under the tenets presented in earlier chapters, the fund theory recognizes cost as related to the creation of equities; and equities are not legal liabilities but restrictions upon assets. A restriction dictated by prudence and forethought in the light of known conditions of undermaintenance (such as might originate from unavailability of materials, of skilled labor, or of time for such operations to be performed—which were common experience during the recent war period) may be just as important financial data as the amount of actual expenditures or legal commitments.

In any event, the report of operations does not pretend to establish an income figure for the year, and the accountant is thus free to report what is reportable and measure what is measurable, to the extent that such information bears upon the problem of financial operations. The reader is not kept in the dark as to the meaning of the charge, since both the expenditures and the estimated undermaintenance are shown; he may use for his purposes whatever data are relevant to his problem, or he may reject any measurement which he deems unsatisfactory or arbitrary. Thus, the computation of income may be made including or excluding this item of estimated undermaintenance.

It may also be objected that the change in residual equity reflects the unrealized appreciation, declination, or other value adjustments, as well as the undermaintenance; and the fund "surplus" is thus inflated or deflated by such items. The answer to this is that we have tried most carefully to avoid in all fund-theory reports any reference to "surplus"[3] as such; and it should be obvious to even the least informed reader of financial statements that the residual equity depends upon, and must be interpreted in the light of, the net assets shown in the same fund. However, if this objection really were sufficiently important as to require special attention in the fund reports, it would be a simple matter to show a specific equity item for unrealized appreciation or declination in the balance sheet and to present the change in this specific equity as a restriction adjustment in the report of operations, as was done with the notes-payable item in the Cash and Banks Fund.

One other point should be mentioned here. The reader may have observed a difference between the items in the General Operating Fund reports and the corresponding items in the conventional balance sheet that was presented as the basis for this illustration. This has to do with the item of wages and interest payable; this appeared on the conventional balance sheet as $408,875 for 19X2, while the same item appeared on the fund balance sheet for the General Operating Fund as $413,000. This difference is intentional; it arises from the treatment, under fund theory, of $4,125 interest payable on bonds held alive in the sinking fund; this $4,125 is shown in the General Operating Fund in the restrictions against general operating assets, although the conventional statement ignores it. The details of this treatment and the reasons for adopting it will appear in the discussion of the sinking-fund reports.

Investment Fund.—The activities of this fund include all those transactions associated with investment operations, such as the acquisition or disposition of bonds and stocks of other companies (including subsidiaries); the collections from, and the recognition of, interest and dividends as they are declared or accrued; and noncurrent loans or advances to subsidiary and affiliated companies. It will be noted, however, that the Investment Fund includes dividends and interest receivable on these investments —items which conventionally are shown among "current" assets. Also, it should be noted that the definition of investments includes both short-term and long-term commitments; that is, those marketable securities which are conventionally shown as current assets appear in the Investment Fund rather than in the General Operating Fund. The reason for this is that the classification of funds is made on the basis of operations; it is not established from the viewpoint of the relative ease with which assets may be converted into cash. The notion of current operations, as exemplified in the General Operating Fund, includes only those activities and transactions which relate directly to the main line of operations—in terms of the major line or lines of product produced and offered for sale.

The only exceptions to this are charges for interest, dividends, and federal taxes; these are really joint transactions, in the sense that they arise from the operations of all the funds together. In theory, such transactions might be allocated to individual funds; this procedure is not followed here for the reason that such an allocation is not practically feasible.

Whether the dollars invested in a given fund are actually or constructively borrowed dollars or whether they arise from another source is a meaningless question; there is no way in which such identifications can be made on an objective basis. What part of a dividend arises from the assets in particular funds is another question which cannot be answered. The allocation of income tax charges is a problem of the same nature; income-tax allocation, however, is even further complicated by the existence of graduated tax rates on brackets of income, the offsetting of losses against gains from other sources, and the effects of timing transactions (as they must be reported for tax purposes) differently from the way in which these items would be treated for other purposes. To all this must be added the fact that, since the fund theory does not concern itself with the income concept (for reasons already explained in previous chapters), there obviously can be no allocation of an income tax between funds.

The more important issue involved in classifying marketable securities, interest, and dividends receivable as investment items is that the operations of investment are distinctly different from those covered by the General Operating Fund; to recognize that investment in other companies and agencies is separate from general operations follows logically from the related managerial activities. When economic capital is invested in other companies, it passes beyond the immediate control of the operating management, and it is therefore segregated from the capital employed in directly controlled activities. Here are the financial reports concerning the Investment Fund:

MYTHICAL CORPORATION

INVESTMENT FUND

COMPARATIVE BALANCE SHEETS, AS AT DECEMBER 31, 19X1 AND 19X2

ASSETS	19X1	19X2	Increase
Interest and dividends receivable	$ 6,000	$ 4,000	$ 2,000*
Bonds of other companies (at cost)	185,000	160,000	25,000*
Unrealized declination of bonds	16,000*	12,000*	4,000
Stocks of other companies (at cost)	248,000	240,000	8,000*
Unrealized appreciation of stocks	33,000	34,000	1,000
Controlling interest in subsidiary company (at cost)	378,000	378,000	....
Unrealized increase in book value of subsidiary's residual equities	22,000	41,000	19,000
Advances to subsidiary company	....	40,000	40,000
Total assets	$856,000	$885,000	$29,000
EQUITIES			
Investment Fund residual equity	$856,000	$885,000	$29,000

* Indicates decrease.

MYTHICAL CORPORATION

INVESTMENT FUND

REPORT OF OPERATIONS, YEAR ENDED DECEMBER 31, 19X2

Financing:				
Proceeds from disposition of bonds of other companies				$20,000
Proceeds, disposition of stocks of other companies				50,000
Collections, interest, and dividends				17,000
Total				87,000
Expenditures:				
New acquisitions of shares of other companies			$32,000	
Loans made to subsidiary company			40,000	72,000
Decrease in fund equity by transfer to Cash and Banks Fund				15,000
Valuations and adjustments:				
Additions to fund equity:				
Interest and dividends accrued receivable			15,000	
Increase in book value of subsidiary company stock			19,000	
Realized appreciation, stocks disposed of:				
Proceeds, per above	$50,000			
Less: Cost when acquired	40,000	$10,000		
Less: Appreciation applicable to prior years		7,000	3,000	
Unrealized appreciation, stocks			8,000	
Reduced unrealized declination of bonds			1,000	
Gross additions to fund equity			46,000	
Deductions from fund equity:				
Realized declination of bonds:				
Proceeds, per above	20,000			
Less: Cost when acquired	25,000	5,000		
Less: Declination, prior years		3,000	2,000	
Net increase in fund equity, exclusive of financing				44,000
Aggregate net increase in fund equity				$29,000

The first major feature to be observed in the statements for the Investment Fund is the presentation of unrealized appreciation and declination of securities held, as measured by market values. Although most accountants would include market-value data as notes or comments within or attached to the financial reports, it is not common practice to add such items into the totals of financial statements. But it seems a bit curious that an accountant who insists upon amortizations of fixed asset charges to avoid the fluctuating "income" that would nearly always result from a cash basis of accounting (even though these amortizations must in the nature of the case be but estimates)—and who is willing to recognize and record appraisals of fixed assets so long as the corresponding depreciation charges are thenceforth computed on the appraised basis[4]—would shy away from similarly spreading so-called capital gains and losses by recognizing market shifts as they occur. It is admitted that market values may at times be capricious in that temporary sags or bulges in the market may result in somewhat abnormal prices on specific dates; but, so long as care is taken to check against such eventualities, market prices are realistic bases of valuation for listed and quoted securities. Especially is this true if, as is the case with the fund reports, there is no representation as to the "income" effect of appreciation or declination; in the fund report there is no reference to "income" as such, especially as regards some "general purpose" calculation.

As was stated above, the fund equity is always subject to interpretation by reviewing the items among the net assets; and, if desired, there might still be set up specific equities to cover the appreciation or declination, so that the fund equity would remain unaffected by appreciation or declination.

The same line of reasoning applies to the treatment accorded in this illustration to the investment in the subsidiary company, with the added argument that an increase in subsidiary company equities is, after all, computed by the same accounting methods and is based upon the identical principles which apply to the reports of the parent-company. Procedures that are satisfactory for determining fund equities in the subsidiary records should be equally acceptable for the valuation of an investment therein, so long as costs are segregated from the computed appreciation or declination. Accounting procedures should not be such as to require the declaration of dividends before the effects of subsidiary operations may appear in the financial reports of the parent; such a procedure merely makes it easier for the true state of affairs to be hidden or misrepresented by shifting the policy with respect to the declaration of subsidiary dividends. It is true that the preparation of consolidated reports would prevent such concealment or misrepresentation; but consolidated reports are not prepared to include every instance of affiliation. This last point applies with special force to those cases in which subsidiaries are effectively controlled by something less than a clear majority of voting stock. Whatever data can be depended upon to add to the information presented in financial reports should be shown therein; this is especially important with respect to affiliated companies and the investments therein.

The effects of presenting data concerning appreciation and declination of investments may be seen in the operating report of the Investment Fund; what would have been (under conventional procedures) a "capital gain" of $5,000 on the sale of investments is shown in the fund report as a current-year adjustment of $1,000 increase and a net prior-years appreciation of $4,000. Although both these amounts are "realized" in the current year, the effects are separated as between current- and prior-years appreciation. Similarly, the recognition of the computed increase in subsidiary company equities represented in the investment account serves to time the effects of subsidiary operations within the period to which they really apply. Dividends received from the subsidiary are here treated so that the realization through dividend declaration is separated from the other effects upon subsidiary fund equities; that is, *both* the dividends and the net increase in equities after dividends appear, but they are separately shown in the operating report. The reader may include either, both, or neither of these figures in the income calculation that he may wish to make.

Another point of interest to be observed in the Investment Fund operating report is that the gross and net shifts in investment position are clearly stated in the "financing" section of the operating report. In this case the net increase in equity by financing transactions is in sharp contrast with the effects of valuations and adjustments. No extant form of financial report presents this information in clear and unequivocal form; although it is conceivable that the conventional statement of income and surplus might be set up to show one part of this information, and the statement of application of funds could be made to show the other part in similar detail, the fund basis of reporting makes it possible to show all these effects in a single statement covering the investment activities and separated from the other areas of operations within the enterprise. In view of the fact that financing transactions (investment and disinvestment) are just as much "operating" transactions as are those conventionally included in statements of income and surplus—sometimes, they are even more indicative of the trend of events or the shifts in policy than are "income" data—there seems to be a real case for attempting to show both classes of data in the same statement.

Sinking Fund.—The transactions in this area of activity are best covered in some detail, because it is here that fund theory brings up some rather interesting points. In this illustration we have assumed a twenty-year bond issue, originally floated at par under an indenture which requires semiannual payments of interest at January 1 and July 1 of each year. To provide for extinguishment of this debt, the indenture calls for annual Sinking Fund contributions of $80,000 each July 1; the trustee is directed to invest available cash by acquiring bonds of this issue, these to be "kept alive in the fund" until their final maturity date; however, should no company bonds be available at satisfactory prices, the trustee may acquire other securities of certain kinds for investment of cash until company bonds may be had under acceptable terms. The explicit transactions of the Sinking Fund to be considered in this illustration are:

July 1, 19X1.—Operations of the Sinking Fund are inaugurated with the receipt of the first $80,000 contribution.

July 2, 19X1.—The trustee acquires $80,000 face amount of company bonds for the fund at a price of $78,050.

December 31, 19X1.—The trustee's fee of $500 is paid.

January 2, 19X2.—Interest coupons are cashed.

July 1, 19X2.—The second $80,000 contribution is received, and interest coupons are cashed.

July 2, 19X2.—$85,000 face amount of bonds of this issue are acquired for $82,780.

December 31, 19X2.—The trustee's fee of $1,000 is paid.

Recording the first year's transactions would involve the following entries:

July 1, 19X1		
Cash in bank	$80,000	
Corporate capital contributions		$80,000
July 2, 19X1		
Reacquired bonds—cost	78,050	
Cash in bank		78,050
December 31, 19X1		
Trustee's fee	500	
Cash in bank		500
Interest accrued receivable	2,000	
Residual equity		2,000
Accumulated discount, reacquired bonds	50	
Residual equity		50

The interest accrual is for one-half year on $80,000 at 5 per cent; the discount accumulation is calculated by spreading the $1,950 discount over nineteen and one-half years, the remaining term of the bonds acquired at July 2. The resulting balance sheet will appear as follows:

MYTHICAL CORPORATION

SINKING FUND

BALANCE SHEET, AT DECEMBER 31, 19X1

ASSETS	
Cash in bank	$ 1,450
Interest accrued receivable	2,000
Reacquired bonds cost	78,050
Discount accumulated on reacquired bonds	50
Total assets	$81,550
EQUITIES	
Corporate capital contributions	$80,000
Residual equity	1,550
Total equities	$81,550

The operating report for this fund would distinguish between financing and valuation and adjustment transactions as indicated below:

MYTHICAL CORPORATION

SINKING FUND

REPORT OF OPERATIONS, YEAR ENDED DECEMBER 31, 19X2

Financing:		
From corporate capital contribution		$80,000
Less: Trustee's fee	$ 500	
Transfer to bond investment	78,050	78,550
Net increase in cash balance		1,450
Transfers, valuations, and adjustments:		
Add: Bonds acquired	78,050	
Discount accumulated on bonds	50	
Interest accrued but not collected	2,000	80,050
Gross increase in Sinking Fund		81,550
Less: Restriction for corporate capital contributions		80,000
Net increase in residual equity		$ 1,550

The second year's transactions would be recorded as follows:

January 2, 19X2

Cash in bank	$ 2,000	
Interest collected		$ 2,000

July 1, 19X2

Cash in bank	80,000	
Corporate capital contributions		80,000
Cash in bank	2,000	
Interest collected		2,000

July 2, 19X2

Reacquired bonds cost	82,780	
Cash in bank		82,780

December 31, 19X2

Trustee's fee	1,000	
Cash in bank		1,000
Interest accrued receivable	2,125	
Residual equity		2,125
Discount accumulation, bonds reacquired	160	
Residual equity		160

The interest entry at December 31 represents the adjustment of "Interest accrued receivable" (which had a balance of $2,000 at January 1) to the proper amount of $4,125, which is one-half year's interest at 5 per cent on $165,000 face amount of bonds. The adjustment for discount is the sum of $100 applicable to bonds acquired in 19X1, and the straight-line accumulation of $2,220 over the eighteen-and-one-half-year remaining term of the bonds acquired in 19X2, which is $120 per year, or $60 for one half-year. The balance sheets may now be presented on a comparative basis for both years:

MYTHICAL CORPORATION

SINKING FUND

COMPARATIVE BALANCE SHEETS, AS AT DECEMBER 31, 19X1 AND 19X2

	19X1	19X2	Increase
ASSETS			
Cash in bank	$ 1,450	$ 1,670	$ 220
Interest accrued receivable	2,000	4,125	2,125
Reacquired bonds cost	78,050	160,830	82,780
Discount accumulations, reacquired bonds	50	210	160
Total assets	$81,550	$166,835	$85,285
EQUITIES			
Corporate capital contributions	$80,000	$160,000	$80,000
Residual equity	1,550	6,835	5,285
Total equities	$81,550	$166,835	$85,285

The operating report for the second year would then appear as shown below:

MYTHICAL CORPORATION

SINKING FUND

REPORT OF OPERATIONS, YEAR ENDED DECEMBER 31, 19X2

Financing:		
From Corporate capital contribution	$80,000	
Interest collected	4,000	$84,000
Less: Trustee's fee	1,000	
Transfer to bond investment	82,780	83,780
Net increase in cash balance		220
Transfers, valuations, and adjustments:		
Additions:		
Interest accrued but not collected	2,125	
Discount accumulated, reacquired bonds	160	
Bonds acquired, cost	82,780	85,065
Gross increase in sinking fund		85,285
Less: Restriction for corporate capital contribution		80,000
Net increase in residual equity		$ 5,285

Some attention should be directed to the accumulation of discount on reacquired bonds. Some accountants would not accept this treatment, nor would they agree to showing the accrued interest receivable as an asset in the Sinking Fund, with the same amount included in the bond interest payable from the General Operating Fund.[5]

This difference in accounting procedure arises from the basic premises of the fund theory as to the structure and purpose of accounting. Under fund theory the Sinking Fund is an accounting unit; the accrual of interest receivable as well as the accumulation of discount on reacquired bonds follow precisely those rules that are applied to the handling of investments generally. And, from the viewpoint of the fund, there is no retirement of these bonds until they are formally delivered to the corporation for final "payment." The actual trust arrangement upon which the Sinking Fund is based then comes to fruition, and the bonds as well as any other assets then in the fund are turned over to the corporation when the trust is discharged. Under the fund theory of accounting it is impossible to bury, as mere transfers of cash, the "interest" on the Sinking Fund bonds, and it is not "correct" to show those bonds as offsets to or direct extinguishments of the main liability.[6]

It is rather interesting to consider from a theoretical viewpoint what might be done in the way of establishing "subfunds" within the Sinking Fund unit; that is, to see what might be accomplished by dividing the Sinking Fund into two smaller units, one to represent the investment aspects of the Sinking Fund, as apart from the current situation with respect to "nonearning" assets. If the Sinking Fund accounts are divided in the general pattern of the double-form balance sheet, and distinctions are maintained between the two subfunds as to the source and disposition of resources, the following comparative balance sheets result from the transactions that have been presented:

MYTHICAL CORPORATION

SINKING FUND

COMPARATIVE BALANCE SHEETS, AS AT DECEMBER 31, 19X1 AND 19X2

(Double-Account Fund)

	19X1	19X2	Increase
Current Account:			
Assets:			
Cash in bank	$ 1,450	$ 1,670	$ 220
Interest accrued receivable	2,000	4,125	2,125
Total assets	$ 3,450	$ 5,795	$ 2,345
Equities:			
Capital invested in current assets	$ 1,950	....	$ 1,950*
Reinvestments in securities	....	$ 830*	830*
Current Fund equity	1,500	6,625	5,125
Total equities	$ 3,450	$ 5,795	$ 2,345
Investment Account:			
Assets:			
Reacquired bonds—cost	$78,050	$160,830	$82,780
Discount accumulated, reacquired bonds	50	210	160
Total assets	$78,100	$161,040	$82,940
Equities:			
Corporate capital contributions	$80,000	$160,000	$80,000
Due from current account	1,950*	....	1,950
Current account reinvestments	....	830	830
Capital Fund equity	50	210	160
Total equities	$78,100	$161,040	$82,940

* Indicates decrease.

Here, it will be observed, the excess of capital contributions over the cost of investments acquired in 19X1 is shown as a restriction in the current account; in the second year, when the investments acquired are $2,780 more than the capital contribution, this restriction disappears; there shows, instead, an item: "Current account reinvestments." Thus, this approach separates the following information not shown by the previous statement: (1) the amount of assets which have arisen from interest collections and accruals, less trustee's fees; (2) the amount of assets arising from discount accumulations, capital gains, and such items; and (3) the effects of transfers of resources as between investment and "floating" assets, including the amount of reinvested interest accretions. In this case the report of operations for the two subfunds would show specifically the cancellation or creation of the "interfund" equities, as resources were transferred between the Current Account and the Investment Account. Of course, if accounting statements are to be prepared on this basis, the accounting entries must be set up to preserve the distinctions implied between the current and the investment sections of the fund. For example, the acquisition of bonds in the second year would be made by entries as follows:

July 2, 19X2

Current Account:		
Capital invested in current assets	$81,950	
Reinvestments in securities	830	
Cash in bank		$82,780
Investment Account:		
Reacquired bonds—cost	82,780	
Due from current account		81,950
Current account reinvestments		830

These entries assume that the receipt of the regular annual contribution of $80,000 on the preceding day was recorded in both subfunds; the current account would have taken up the cash with a credit to "capital invested in current assets," and the investment entry would have shown the amount as "Due from current account," credited to "Corporate capital contributions." The suggested refinement is perhaps not worth the additional trouble of extra entries and postings; the subfund situation does, however, apply the principles mentioned previously with rather interesting effect.

Capital Fund.—The Capital Fund for this illustration is defined in the same terms as in the preceding chapters; that is, this fund includes all long-term assets and equities (and their corresponding interim accounts) which are not specifically assigned to some other fund. The form of the operating report is the same as has been employed for other funds in this illustration, and the comparative balance sheets are drawn up to show the long-term investment position with special emphasis upon fixed assets, depreciation and amortization and other reserves, and the long-term financial structure.

MYTHICAL CORPORATION

CAPITAL FUND

COMPARATIVE BALANCE SHEETS, AS AT DECEMBER 31, 19X1 AND 19X2

	19X1	19X2	Increase
ASSETS			
Land, buildings, and equipment—cost	$4,488,000	$4,782,000	$ 294,000
Allowance for depreciation	1,124,000	1,231,000	107,000
Total assets	$3,364,000	$3,551,000	$ 187,000
EQUITIES			
5 per cent Sinking Fund bonds payable	$1,000,000	$1,000,000	....
8 per cent preferred stock, $100 par	1,300,000	....	$1,300,000*
Common stock, no par value	1,200,000	2,710,000	1,510,000
Reserve for additional war costs	....	200,000	200,000
Reserve for maintenance and repairs	280,000	328,000	48,000
Residual equity	416,000*	687,000*	271,000*
Total equities	$3,364,000	$3,551,000	$ 187,000

* Indicates decrease or deduction.

MYTHICAL CORPORATION

CAPITAL FUND

REPORT OF OPERATIONS, YEAR ENDED DECEMBER 31, 19X2

Financing:			
Expenditures, retirement of preferred stock		$1,353,000	
Additions to plant assets		626,000	
Repairs and maintenance reserve		93,000	$2,072,000
Proceeds, additional common stock issued		1,360,000	
Retirement and sale of plant assets		27,000	1,387,000*
Increase in residual equity through financing			685,000
Transfers, valuations, and adjustments:			
Additions:			
Adjustment, overdepreciation of plant assets retired		6,000	
Deductions:			
Call premium and other costs, preferred-stock retirement	$ 53,000		
Dividends issued in common shares	150,000		
Transfer to reserve for additional war costs	200,000		
Transfer of long-term plant cost to be absorbed in operations as depreciation	418,000		
Adjustment of reserve for maintenance and repair	141,000	962,000*	
Net total transfers, valuations, and adjustments (deduct)			956,000*
Net decrease in residual equity			$ 271,000*

* Indicates decrease or deduction.

It will be observed that there is a net debit balance in the residual equity of the Capital Fund for both 19X1 and 19X2. At first sight, this deficit appears anomalous; for, if equities are restrictions upon assets, how can there be an excess of restrictions over assets in this fund unless there have been large "capital losses"? However, a little reflection will reveal that this debit balance is really a significant figure; it reflects the net result of some important financial activities. Actually, this debit balance is a receivable from other funds; moreover, it implies that there really ought to be recognized, in some other fund or funds, specific-equity restrictions of the same amount.

This balance arises from the following: Initial financing of a business practically always involves the creation of long-term equities against the assets thus procured; although such financing commonly provides for the acquisition of long-term assets, there is usually raised in the same process a certain amount of working capital. The Capital Fund of a new enterprise would thus normally show a debit balance for assets transferred to working capital funds, and there would also appear in the funds to which those assets were transferred specific equities of the same total amount. Now, as operations bring new resources into the working capital funds, the management may begin to consider the possibility of plant expansion—at least, there will arise expenditures for repairs, maintenance, renovations, additions, or betterments of plant assets. To the extent that these

Capital Fund expenditures exceed transfers from the Capital Fund to cover depreciation or amortization, the net expansion in fixed assets is being financed from operating revenues—or, as the phrase is, "surplus is being plowed back." Thus, there may be an eventual offsetting of the original debit balance; but, until this does occur, the debit balance will remain in the Capital Fund to call attention to the net advance of long-term capital for other purposes. Even though (as in this case) the appropriate restrictions are not set up in the working capital funds (general operating, cash and banks, or investment funds), the debit balance in the Capital Fund cannot be waved aside or overlooked. The extent to which surplus has actually been plowed back into capital assets is thus clearly seen in the balance sheets of the Capital Fund from year to year. The presentation of this debit balance makes it possible to see just what financial flows have occurred and what their effects have been; these important financial operations are not buried within a general (and usually confusing and meaningless) "surplus" of the conventional variety. Not only are the ebbs and flows of financial resources seen clearly in the report of operations when they occur but, in addition, the cumulative effect of such transactions is preserved in the residual balance in the Capital Fund. Of course, there should be some reduction in the residual equities in the working capital funds, so that the aggregate fund equities will not be overstated; in such case, this debit balance is treated as an advance to other funds, and there will be no residual equity in the Capital Fund. In this illustration this could be done only arbitrarily by adjustment of the balance sheets. Actually, however, the maintenance of appropriate records would indicate precisely which fund equities should be reduced and just where the specific equities to restrict working capital funds for advances from capital should appear. The effect would be to state working capital surpluses in such a way as to make clear the amount and the kinds of assets available for specific purposes, such as the disbursement of dividends, the expansion of plant, or an increase in investment in certain areas of activity.

The consolidated reports.—It may still be maintained that to show detailed information concerning individual funds may have some merit but that such procedure provides no one place in which the over-all effects of the operations may be seen together; that is, that fund-reporting does not fit the data together into a summary presentation for the enterprise as a whole. It is true that the use of individual reports for each of the funds prevents this. However, as has been pointed out, the definition of a fund is flexible. Funds once established may be divided (as was suggested in the treatment of sinking-fund operations), or they may be combined into larger units whenever it may be desirable. Thus, in the present case, it is entirely feasible to "consolidate" these reports in the sense of bringing together the information they present in summary terms. The "Consolidated Report of Fund Operations" of the Mythical Corporation appears on pp. 118–19.

The consolidated operating report shows in summary form all the details which have been presented in the reports for individual funds. Thus, it serves to give an over-all view of not only the transactions ordinarily shown in conventional statements of income and surplus, but it presents also the ways in which resources placed at the disposal of the

CONSOLIDATED REPORT OF FUND OPER

	Cash and Banks Fund		General Operating Fund	
	Increase	Decrease	Increase	Decrease
Financing transactions:				
Collections from trade customers	$24,065,000			$24,065,000
Bank loans	500,000	$ 500,000		
Proceeds, disposal of investments	70,000			
Interest and dividends collected	17,000			
Additional common shares issued	1,360,000			
Retirement and sale of plant assets	27,000			
Expenditures for:				
Materials, supplies, and miscellaneous		14,759,000	$14,759,000	
Wages and interest		6,633,000	6,633,000	
Local, state, and federal taxes		1,577,000	1,577,000	
Cash dividends, preferred stock		104,000	104,000	
Cash dividends, common stock		272,000	272,000	
Acquisitions of securities		32,000		
Loans to subsidiary company		40,000		
Annual contribution to sinking fund		80,000		
Acquisitions of bonds—sinking fund				
Additions to plant assets		626,000		
Retirement of preferred stock		1,353,000		
Repairs and maintenance		93,000		
Trustee's fee—sinking fund				
Total	$26,039,000	$26,069,000	$23,345,000	$24,065,000
Net equity changes from financing transactions		$ 30,000		$ 720,000
Transfers, valuations, and adjustments:				
Add: Net revenue from sales			$24,595,000	
Interest and dividends accrued				
Net realized appreciation, investments sold				
Accumulation of discount, sinking-fund bonds				
Overdepreciation of plant assets retired				
Overallowance for uncollectibles, prior year			3,000	
Unrealized appreciation of securities (net)				
Less: Operating expenses (per schedule)				$22,370,000
Interest charges on bonds and payables				64,000
Inventory appreciation, prior year				157,000
Inventory declination, current year				135,000
Provisions for local, state, and federal taxes				1,062,000
Cash dividends declared				376,000
Call premium and other costs, preferred stock retired				
Stock dividends issued in common shares				
Transfer to reserve, additional war costs				
Interfund cost transfers:				
Depreciation and amortization			418,000	
Estimated maintenance and repairs			141,000	
Total			$25,157,000	$24,164,000
Net equity changes, from transfers, valuations and adjustments			$ 993,000	
Total combined net changes in fund equities		$ 30,000	$ 273,000	

CORPORATION

ATIONS, YEAR ENDED DECEMBER 31, 19X2

Investment Fund		Sinking Fund—Current		Sinking Fund—Investments		Capital Fund	
Increase	Decrease	Increase	Decrease	Increase	Decrease	Increase	Decrease
	$70,000						
	17,000	$ 4,000					
							$1,360,000
							27,000
$32,000							
40,000							
		80,000			$80,000		
			$82,780	$82,780			
						$ 626,000	
						1,353,000	
						93,000	
			1,000				
$72,000	$87,000	$84,000	$83,780	$82,780	$80,000	$2,072,000	$1,387,000
	$15,000	$ 220		$ 2,780		$ 685,000	
$15,000		$ 2,125					
1,000							
				$ 160			
						$ 6,000	
28,000							
							$ 53,000
							150,000
							200,000
							418,000
							141,000
$44,000		$ 2,125		$ 160		$ 6,000	$ 962,000
$44,000		$ 2,125		$ 160			956,000
$29,000		$ 2,345		$ 2,940			$ 271,000

management have been employed, in terms of transfers and financing transactions. This report supersedes—actually, it includes—the statement of cash receipts and disbursements, the statement of funds, and the various analyses of reserve accounts that must all be at hand to supplement the statement of income and surplus if a clear picture of the operating results is to be had. This report and the balance sheets of the individual funds serve together to present the panorama of operating activities in clear perspective. One interesting aspect of the consolidated operating report should be noted: had the fund statements been combined (as distinguished from "consolidated" in the sense in which that term is here employed), the effect would have been to eliminate most of the financing transactions. Thus a single report for the enterprise as a whole cannot show the information to be had from the consolidated fund report. This fact is the basic reason for preparing the conventional statement of funds; only in some specially designed statement can the financing transactions be shown for the firm as a whole. But the statement of funds is but an inadequate and crude analysis, as compared with what can be done by fund-reporting, which separates and at the same time preserves the details of financing transactions.

The operating report as presented on a fund basis is useful not only because it serves to bring together certain kinds of data which cannot be presented in conventional statements for the firm as a whole but also because it serves to draw the attention of the reader to the real information it contains. Because there is no emphasis upon any isolated or summary figure in the report, the reader cannot seize upon some one figure (usually an inadequate one) to serve his purpose. Since he cannot employ such a short cut to a judgment as to the effects of operations, he is led (even though unwillingly) to *read* and *study* the report, paying attention to the real information which is presented therein. After such a reading, and with some basis for selecting the important things in the presentation, the reader will be in a better position to combine relevant items and to evaluate them with respect to his specific problem. There is really no other way to an intelligent use of accounting data. The accountant should not suggest, in the form of his reports or otherwise, that problems can be solved by the use of summary or general purpose figures. The responsibility of the accountant is to compile and present such information as records, measurements, or other sources may make available to enable the reader to see what happened and how it came about. But there this responsibility ceases; it does not extend to pointing up the results of qualification in terms of a single and final figure designed to meet some undefined or "general" purpose.

The Consolidated Fund balance sheets are not presented here, because they would show precisely the same information as appears in the individual fund statements. But there is some point to indicating how these data would be displayed. If the balance sheets are arranged so as to deduct from the total assets of each fund the sums of the relevant specific equities, the residual equity will appear as the net "balance" of each fund. If these fund balances are then summarized, the total will show the conventional "surplus" for whatever that figure may be worth. For instance, in the present case the fund equities would be totaled as follows:

MYTHICAL CORPORATION

SUMMARIZATION OF RESIDUAL EQUITIES AS AT DECEMBER 31, 19X2

	Balance per Fund Balance Sheet	Increase or Decrease during Year 19X2
Cash and Banks Fund	$ 912,000	$ 30,000*
General Operating Fund	3,229,000	273,000
Investment Fund	885,000	29,000
Sinking Fund—current	6,625	5,125
Sinking Fund—investments	210	160
Capital Fund	687,000*	271,000*
Total	$4,345,835	$ 6,285

* Indicates decrease.

This tabulation is a bit startling, since the original (conventional) balance sheet showed an unrestricted earned surplus equity at December 31, 19X2, amounting to $4,581,795, and the increase in this account during the year was shown as $346,345. The differences are the result of measuring and timing transactions under two methods of accounting: those embraced by entity and fund theories. The following reconciliations show those differences in detail:

RECONCILIATION OF INITIAL EQUITIES AT JANUARY 1, 19X2

Unrestricted earned surplus balance, per conventional balance sheet		$4,225,450
Summary of equities, fund balance sheets:		
Cash and Banks Fund	$ 942,000	
General Operating Fund	2,956,000	
Investment Fund	856,000	
Sinking Fund—current equity	1,500	
Sinking Fund—investment equity	50	
Capital Fund	416,000*	4,339,550
Difference fund equities over conventional equity		$ 114,100
Items accounting for this difference:		
Fund equity greater than conventional equity:		
Unrealized appreciation, inventory	157,000	
Unrealized appreciation, investments	39,000	
Discount accumulation, sinking fund	50	$ 196,050
Fund equity less than conventional equity:		
Sinking Fund contribution restricted	80,000	
Gain on retirement of bonds in Sinking Fund	1,950	81,950
Net difference accounted for		$ 114,100

RECONCILIATION OF EQUITY CHANGES DURING 19X2

Equity increase, per conventional statements	$356,345
Equity increase per fund reports	6,285
Difference, conventionally reported increase over that reported per fund statements	$350,060
Items accounting for this difference:	
Fund equity increase less than conventional increase:	
Realization of inventory appreciation, prior year	$157,000
Provision for inventory declination, current year	135,000
Sinking Fund transfer shown as restricted equity	80,000
Realization of prior years' appreciation of securities	4,000
Gain on retirement of bonds in Sinking Fund	2,220
Total	378,220
Less: Fund equity increase greater than conventional increase:	
Unrealized appreciation of investments	28,000
Accumulation of discount, Sinking Fund bonds	160
Total	28,160
Net difference accounted for	$350,060

RECONCILIATION OF EQUITY TOTALS AT DECEMBER 31, 19X2

Unrestricted earned surplus, per conventional balance sheet	$4,581,795
Summary of fund equities, per fund balance sheets	4,345,835
Difference	$ 235,960
Excess of conventional surplus increase over fund-equity increases, per computation above	$ 350,060
Less: Difference between initial surplus and initial fund equities, as per preceding calculation	114,100
Difference in final equities accounted for	$ 235,960

The differences that are here summarized represent viewpoints toward basic theory; one theory underlies each set of reports, and the merits of one or the other must stand or fall on the case which has been presented for them. But quite apart from those items, the fact remains that fund theory does provide at least a form of financial report which could be employed with other valuations and with other criteria for timing the transactions. It would be a simple matter indeed to adjust those items which make up the difference between the conventional amounts and those arrived at through the fund approach. The forms of reports that have appeared here are entirely independent of different bases of valuation and different criteria for timing the effects of transactions, and financial reports might be set up in these arrangements whether or not the fund theory is accepted in full. However, the same form of presentation does not assure the same results.

As they have been presented here, these financial summaries serve to present certain kinds of information which logically could not be included under the premises of entity or proprietary theories of accounting. Rather, the fund theory seeks to employ the most flexible and most inclusive bases for compiling and reporting all financial data that are recorded or can be measured in some reasonably objective way. In this the aim is to present in the reports whatever alternative information can be compiled, so that the reader may be able at least partially to meet whatever purpose or problem he may have in mind. The fund theory espouses no "personalistic" interest but strives for a detached point of view from which to analyze and report financial operations; but it is the *reader* of the statements who must decide how the financial data bear upon given situations or how they should be combined to serve various purposes. Unless such a viewpoint is adopted and maintained, the financial statements will inevitably exclude some data that may be important; what is worse, the reader may be given only that part of the whole story which serves some end other than the one in which he has a stake. If accounting data are to serve the many uses to which they are being put, and if accounting reports are to be really informative and helpful in furthering those uses, the fund theory offers distinct advantages over conventionally accepted ideologies.

However, in the final analysis no theory can ever serve of itself to do more than correlate and integrate ideas; whether any such frame of reference or structure of thought is really useful can only be settled in the laboratories of accounting practice. However, in setting the design for those experiments which may be used to test the ideas presented herein, the practitioner should be ever mindful of Canning's statement:

> It ought never to be forgotten that those who are capable of profiting by all the information the accountant is capable of giving are a very small number indeed. Nor should it be forgotten that the number who look to the accountant for help and protection is very great. The accountant forgets neither of these things.[7]

NOTES

CHAPTER I

1. George O. May, Financial Accounting (New York: Macmillan Co., 1943), p. vii; see also Stephen Gilman, Accounting Concepts of Profit (New York: Ronald Press Co., 1939), pp. 8-9 et passim.

2. Arthur David Ritchie, Scientific Method (New York: Harcourt, Brace & Co., 1923), p. 156.

3. It seems agreed that nothing worthy of the name of theory existed in the field of accounting prior to 1800. Edward A. Peragallo (Origin and Evolution of Double-Entry Bookkeeping [New York: American Institute Publishing Co., 1938]) writes: "No theory of accounting was devised from the time of Paciolo down to the opening of the nineteenth century. Suggestions of theory appear here and here, but not to the extent necessary to place accountancy on a systematic basis ....there grew up instead a great mass of rules applicable to particular cases" (p. 92).

A similar position is taken by A. C. Littleton, in his Accounting Evolution to 1900 (New York: American Institute Publishing Co., 1933): "Discussions of proprietorship which went beyond the customary explanation of entries for capital invested or withdrawn or entries for closing profit and loss to capital were, even in the nineteenth century, the exception rather than the rule. There still was a disinclination on the part of most writers to put 'theory' in their books....yet there were a few who began to break away from the old pattern.....Their speculations concerning the fundamental nature of double-entry bookkeeping (probably the real beginning of theory) soon led them to proprietorship as the keystone of the arch" (pp. 165-66).

4. Littleton (op. cit., p. 193) would seem to disagree with this statement, for he writes: "Continental writers of the last decade of the nineteenth century labored under the impression that the origin of the entity theory reached back only into the eighties. But later researches tend to show that the basis at least extends much further back than that period." However, the references that are discussed seem to be but minor ones, until Folsom's treatise, dated 1873. Later (p. 200) Littleton states: "It can hardly be said that the entity theory had achieved its full stature as an organized exposition of the nature of double-entry bookkeeping prior to 1900. Much that was necessary to round out the early notions was added after the turn of the century."

5. The present discussion will not attempt to present all the details of either the proprietary or the entity position; this has been done as well as it may be by those writers who have espoused one or the other cause. Emphasis will here be given only to those aspects of entity and proprietary theory as bear upon our exposition of the fund view of accounting.

6. C. E. Sprague, The Philosophy of Accounts (New York: Ronald Press Co., 1913), p. 46; cited by Gilman, op. cit., p. 50.

7. W. A. Paton and A. C Littleton, An Introduction to Corporate Accounting Standards (Chicago: American Accounting Association, 1940), p. 8.

8. Ibid., p. 9.

9. Gilman, op. cit., p. 74.

10. Ibid., p. 55.

11. W. A. Paton, Advanced Accounting (New York: Macmillan Co., 1941), p. 322.

12. See Paton and Littleton, op. cit., pp. 11-16, 23, 24-45, et passim.

13. W. A. Paton, Accounting Theory (New York: Ronald Press Co., 1922), p. 19.

14. Ibid., p. 473; Gilman, op. cit., pp. 47, 51, 246, et passim; Paton and Littleton, op. cit., pp. 8-9.

15. George R. Husband, "The Corporate Entity Fiction and Accounting Theory," Accounting Review, XIII, No. 3 (September, 1938), 242.

16. Warner H. Hord, "A Neglected Area of Accounting Valuation," Accounting Review, XVII, No. 4 (October, 1942), 337.

17. Littleton, op. cit., pp. 46-61.

18. Paton, Accounting Theory, p. iv.

19. John B. Canning, The Economics of Accountancy (New York: Ronald Press Co., 1929), p. 55.

20. Op. cit., p. 252.

21. Op. cit., p. 50.

22. Paton and Littleton, op. cit., p. 9.

23. G. A. McFarland and R. D. Ayars, Accounting Fundamentals (New York: McGraw-Hill Book Co., 1936), p. 179. The identical statement appears also on p. 394.

24. C Reinold Noyes, "A Consolidated Balance Sheet for a Democracy," Journal of Accountancy, LXXXIII, No. 2 (February, 1947), 100-112, refers to this meaning of fund: "'Fund' is the term suggested in the author's Institution of Property, pp. 469 ff., for any 'legally segregated organic grouping of property.' Jurisprudence has had no precise term, or even concept for the purpose, though the term 'estate' has sometimes been used in this broader sense" (p. 103).

25. Hord, op. cit., p. 337. (My italics.)

26. W. A. Paton, Essentials of Accounting (New York: Macmillan Co., 1938), p. 35. (My italics.)

CHAPTER II

1. Cf. P. W. Bridgman, The Logic of Modern Physics (New York: Macmillan Co., 1928), p. 10: "The operations by which length is measured should be uniquely specified. If we have more than one set of operations, we have more than one concept, and strictly there should be a separate name to correspond to each different set of operations." See also Bridgman's Nature of Physical Theory (Princeton: Princeton University Press, 1936), p. 16: "Science, language, and rational thought are devices by means of which I try to make adjustments, and I have to find out by experiment whether these are successful devices."

2. W A. Paton, Essentials of Accounting (New York: Macmillan Co., 1938), p. 23.

3. W. A. Paton and A. C. Littleton, An Introduction to Corporate Accounting Standards (Chicago: American Accounting Association, 1940), pp. 25-26.

4. It is possible to go even further than this and to insist that the meaning of a quantitative concept is to be found in the measurement-operations. Bridgman (The Logic of Modern Physics, p. 5) suggests that "length is as much and nothing more than the set of operations by which length is determined." But see below, n. 9.

5. One of the interesting examples of this "homogeneity of substance" is exemplified by temperature measurements. Despite the fact that temperature is measured by what may seem to be indirect means, and also despite the problems that are involved in handling the numerous independent variables that affect such measurements, it has been established empirically that all substances (thus far subjected to test) which do not ionize in solution depress the freezing-point of a solution by .186°C. per gram molecular weight of solute. This certainly suggests an underlying homogeneity in the many phenomena that are related to such a situation.

6. W. A. Paton and A. C. Littleton, An Introduction to Corporate Accounting Standards (Chicago: American Accounting Association, 1940), p. 26.

7. Frank H. Knight, "Capitalistic Production, Time and the Rate of Return" (University of Chicago, Department of Economics, 1938), p. 2. (Mimeographed.)

8. Alfred Marshall, Principles of Economics (8th ed.; London: Macmillan & Co., 1930), pp. 92 ff.

9. All quantifications are abstractions made in the interest of objectivity (social consensus). Although it is true that, in Dantzig's phrase, the subjective world contains no number concept, but the objective world contains nothing that is free of it--this is merely saying that abstraction of the right kind contributes to communication and objective validity. Counting differs from measurement in the way in which abstraction enters--in counting, the unit is defined subjectively (by one person); in measurement, the unit is defined objectively (conventionally, as a standard); in any event, the number series is useful because it is a conventionalized abstraction. Measurement and counting both involve the recognition of some attribute or group of attributes that can be correlated with the number series. Without

conventional acceptance, the number abstraction is meaningless; the recognition of attributes, as well as the interpretation of a quantification, are both impossible unless there exists some body of experience or pattern of thought through whose conventional acceptance communication may be achieved.

Although theories to some extent may be conditioned by the exigencies of measurement, the measurement depends upon the theory in the first instance. Therefore, the position taken by Bridgman (length is but its measurement) cannot be accepted without reservations. The requirement of homogeneity of substance in concepts arises from the fact that unrelated measurements may confuse rather than inform, unless such homogeneity exists.

As indicated previously, we are not here concerned primarily with the problems of measuring the things with which accounting deals. The problem of joint relations (joint services, and joint cost) alone makes the problem of accounting measurements a difficult one. We prefer for present purposes to establish the theoretical basis on qualitative grounds, reserving the problems of measurement in accounting for some later and more extensive study.

10. *Op. cit.*, p. 13.

11. John B. Canning, *The Economics of Accountancy* (New York: Ronald Press Co., 1929), p. 188. Later (pp. 248-309) Canning applies this theory to the valuation aspects of accounting.

12. *Ibid.*, p. 14.

13. Paton and Littleton, *op. cit.*, pp. 13-14.

14. Cf. Paton, *op. cit.*, pp. 52-53.

15. J. M. Clark, *Studies in the Economics of Overhead Costs* (Chicago: University of Chicago Press, 1923), pp. 35-67; W. B. McFarland, "The Economics of Business Costs," *Accounting Review*, XV, No. 2 (June, 1940), 196-204; E. B Wilcox, "What Is Cost?" *Accounting, Auditing, and Taxes, 1941: Papers Presented at the Fifty-fourth Annual Meeting of the American Institute of Accountants* (New York: American Institute of Accountants, 1941). On p. 101 of this article appears the statement: "To understand what cost is, it is necessary to understand that it is not definite."

16. J. C. Bonbright, *The Valuation of Property* (New York: McGraw-Hill Book Co., 1937), I, 12: "As with other terms (like income and cost) so with value--the very meaning of the term is conditioned by the methodology of estimating its amount."

17. Paton, *op. cit.*, p. 713.

18. Although the "Appropriations" account balance is not shown on the balance sheet of a fund at the close of a fiscal period, it does appear on interim statements. The "Reserve for Encumbrances" does appear on both interim and final statements; this account does not represent a liability in any sense except a contingent or conditional one (Lloyd Morey, *Introduction to Governmental Accounting* [New York: John Wiley & Sons, 1932], pp. 29, 38-39; C H. Chatters and Irving Tenner, *Municipal and Governmental Accounting* [New York: Prentice-Hall, Inc., 1940], pp. 100, 531). It is interesting to observe that the right-hand side of the balance sheet is captioned "Liabilities, Appropriations, Reserves, and Surplus" in Chatters and Tenner, *op. cit.*, p. 39.

19. A. C. Littleton, *Accounting Evolution to 1900* (New York: American Institute Publishing Co., 1933), pp. 165-91.

20. *Ibid.*, pp. 192- 203; Stephen Gilman, *Accounting Concepts of Profit* (New York: Ronald Press Co., 1939), pp. 48-50 *et passim*.

21. Warner H. Hord, "A Neglected Area of Accounting Valuation," *Accounting Review*, XVII (October, 1942), 337: "'Asset' and 'equity' essentially describe different aspects of a single business property....thus, the term 'property' will imply an asset element and an equity element of equal amount and identical origin."

CHAPTER III

1. William J. Vatter, "Limitations of Overhead Allocation," *Accounting Review*, XX, No. 2 (April, 1945), 163-76.

2. The fund concept of expense is analogous to physical concepts in the fields of illumination, hydrodynamics, or electronics. Although there may be a demonstrable unit in the form of particles (droplets, electrons), the physical ideas are framed in terms of a general flow (current, beam, or stream). The reason for framing these concepts in terms of flow is

found in the fact that criteria can be applied to determine the presence or absence of a flow with some degree of ease; the criteria necessary to trace the movement of individual particles are much more difficult to apply. This is not the same thing as saying that the concept is determined by the process of measurement; the existence of criteria for recognizing a phenomenon does not require or imply measurement of it.

3. W. A. Paton, *Essentials of Accounting* (New York: Macmillan Co., 1938), p. 81.

4. James L. Dohr, "Income Divorced from Reality," *Journal of Accountancy*, LXVI, No. 6 (December, 1938), 362.

5. These writers point out that assets may be augmented from five sources--financing, gains from liquidation of items not stock in trade, gifts and discoveries, revaluations, and furnishing of product. They go on to say that "only the last of these should be recognized as the *primary* source of revenue," remarking that the price aggregate of the sale transaction expresses revenue (W. A. Paton and A. C. Littleton, *An Introduction to Corporate Accounting Standards* [Chicago: American Accounting Association, 1940], pp. 47-48).

6. The so-called "cash basis" of reporting revenue from instalment sales is really more of an accrual concept than it would seem, since it involves a definite pattern of cost-allocation or expense measurement (Paton, *op. cit.*, pp. 600-605). Paton says that the cash basis is a relatively complex type of accounting and should be employed only in circumstances where a strong case can be made for its use. In those instances where a *strict* cash basis of accounting is used the terms "revenue" and "expense" are simply irrelevant; they should be replaced by "cash receipts" and "disbursements."

7. To deny this is to negate the entire structure of accrual accounting; although there may be reason to apply tests such as "realization," "earning," or "availability," we prefer to discuss these after the main point has been developed.

8. This takes cognizance of the fact that some bonds do not have terminal dates but are established by indenture to run indefinitely. Such securities are perhaps to be distinguished from bonds with maturity dates, but the fact reamins that there is an ultimate obligation to repay at least the face value of the bond if the enterprise is terminated.

9. J. M. Keynes, *A Treatise on Money* (New York: Harcourt Brace & Co., 1930), p. 53.

10. R. P. Marple, *Capital Surplus and Corporate Net Worth* (New York: Ronald Press Co., 1936), pp. 111-27. The author points out that revaluations usually involve one or more of the following: (1) past errors in allocation of service charges as between asset and expense categories; (2) changes in the demand for the given service potentials that are revalued; (3) shifts in the purchasing power of money.

11. Cf. the position taken by Gilman (*Accounting Concepts of Profit* [New York: Ronald Press Co., 1939], p. 111): "When property is donated to the business as an outright gift, it should theoretically not give rise to any entry. *The value parted with having been zero, the value received is also zero.*" (My italics.) It would seem that Gilman would deny the possibility of accounting income in every situation; for if values received must be considered as equal to values parted with, there is not much opportunity for profit, income, or gain in any sense!

12. C H. Chatters and Irving Tenner, *Municipal and Government Accounting* (New York: Prentice-Hall, Inc., 1940), p. 10.

13. Roy B. Kester, *Principles of Accounting* (4th ed.; New York: Ronald Press Co., 1939), p. 17.

14. *Ibid.*, p. 462.

15. George R. Husband and Olin E. Thomas, *Principles of Accounting* (Boston: Houghton Mifflin Co., 1935), p. 543.

16. W. A. Paton, *Advanced Accounting* (New York: Macmillan Co., 1941), pp. 453-55.

17. W. A. Paton, *Accounting Theory* (New York: Ronald Press Co., 1922), p. 446.

18. *Op. cit.*, p. 104.

19. *Ibid.*, p. 102 (My italics.)

20. *Ibid.*, p. 7.

21. *Ibid.*, p. 103.

22. Ibid., p. 105.

23. H. A. Finney, Principles of Accounting (New York: Prentice-Hall, Inc., 1936), I, 117.

24. Paton, Advanced Accounting, p. 441.

25. Cf. Martin Taitel, Profits, Productive Activities, and New Investment ("T.N.E.C. Monograph," No. 12 [Washington, D.C.: Government Printing Office, 1941), pp. 4-8.

26. W. A. Paton, Recent and Prospective Developments in Accounting Theory ("Harvard University Business Research Studies," No. 25, Vol. XXVII, No. 2 [Boston, March, 1940]), p. 11: "Modern Accounting essays the difficult task of breaking the continuing stream of business operations into time sections. The result, at the best, is no more than a series of careful estimates. To prepare an income statement for a particular month, quarter, or year requires the severing of many living threads; each report is tentative in that its final validatinn depends in part at least upon future events. It is no wonder that Justice Brandeis and others have suggested that there can be no wholly dependable computation of net income until the particular enterprise has run its course."

27. "Accounting Principles Affecting Corporate Reports," Accounting Review, XI, No. 2 (June, 1936), 187-91. Especially to be noted is the following: "With the emphasis given to statements of corporate earnings 'per share' and to other measures of corporate performance, a common yardstick is demanded. Since it is not possible to measure precisely at the end of any year all the values which have been acquired or dissipated during that year, it becomes important to encompass within a single statement, not only the best possible measures for the year's results, but also the best possible measure of such corrections as seem necessary in the statements already made for prior periods" (p. 190). Also to be noted is: "The income statement for any given period should reflect all revenues properly given accounting recognition and all costs written off during the period, regardless of whether or not they are the results of operations during that period; to the end that for any period of years in the history of the enterprise the assembled income statements will express completely all gains and losses" (p 189), This latter pronouncement establishes the content of the income statement largely in terms of the bookkeeping entries made during the period. In this, the significance of "income" is certainly not clear.

28. Research Bulletin No. 8 (February, 1941), p. 63: "There are decided advantages in such combined statements, but also some disadvantages. The committee therefore feels that a useful purpose will be served if it expresses approval of the practice where it is found feasible, without recommending its general adoption."

29. T. H. Sanders, "Accounting Research: Objectives and Methods," Accounting Review, XV, No. 1 (March, 1940), 87.

30. Paton, Recent and Prospective Developments in Accounting Theory, p. 16.

31. Arundel Cotter, Fool's Profits (New York: Barron's Publishing Co., 1940), p. 30.

32. Paton, Advanced Accounting, p. 453.

CHAPTER IV

1. Principles of College and University Business Practice ("American Council on Education Studies," Series III: Financial Advisory Service, Vol. I, No. 9 [July, 1937]), pp. 3-4. Quoted by Edward V. Miles, Jr., Manual of Teachers College Accounting (Washington: American Council on Education, 1940), pp. 4-5.

2. Municipal Accounting Statements (Chicago: National Committee on Municipal Accounting, 1941), p. 1.

3. Ibid., p. 5.

4. C. H. Chatters and Irving Tenner, Municipal and Government Accounting (New York: Prentice-Hall, Inc., 1940), pp. 150-57. Although these authors do not employ the term "fund" in connection with fixed assets or bonded debt, they do point out clearly that the accounts for general bonded indebtedness and for fixed assets are to be considered as "separate groups of accounts." However, the Accountant's Handbook, pp. 1330-31, shows a "capital fund" in a municipal balance sheet in which both fixed assets and long-term debt are shown together.

5. National Committee on Municipal Accounting, op. cit., p. 5.

6. The lack of emphasis on valuation issues probably does arise from the absence--or at least the lesser importance--of "profits" in the government and institution operations. The Accountant's Handbook says: "Ascertaining income or profit is generally not an objective of the accounting records of governmental units. Costs should be appropriately classified and controlled but the matching of expenditures with the sources from which the funds have been derived to obtain an operating balance is not a very significant process in typical government activities. . . . . The primary concern of the financial administrators of the government unit is to procure sufficient cash to provide the services expected from the unit" (p. 1278).

This aspect of the case, however, seems to the present writer to be somewhat inconclusive; although profits may not be the goal of institutional or governmental activities, the matching of costs and revenues is still important. "Breaking even" is itself only a special case of profit accounting, and, while the profit motive may have little bearing on this situation, the aims of solvency and continued effectiveness of operations have at least a very similar effect.

7. Op. cit., p. 201.

8. Above, chap. 1, nn. 10-12.

9. Op. cit., p. 202.

10. Interim balance sheets will show not only the encumbrances but the appropriations which apply to the fund; and although the appropriations lapse at the end of the fiscal period and are thus absent from the final balance sheet, outstanding and unliquidated commitments appear as a regular item, "Reserve for Encumbrances."

11. Op. cit., p. 201.

12. Ibid., pp. 40, 70-71, 64-65, 46-47.

13. W. A. Paton, Advanced Accounting (New York: Ronald Press Co., 1922), pp. 8-9; see also Carman G. Blough, "Developments in Accounting and Auditing," Journal of Accountancy, LXXX, No. 2 (February, 1945), 107.

14. The line of argument that is advanced against the recognition of depreciation as expense in government and institution accounting is generally presented in the pattern adopted by Frederick J. Haller, Suggestions for an Accounting Plan for a Non-profit Organization--the Y.W.C.A. (New York: Womans Press, 1936), p. 23: "In respect to buildings and equipment used for association purposes, it is generally considered sufficient to charge each year against the cost of operations only the amount required to make all repairs and replacements to maintain the properties in first class condition during the current year. On the basis of the experience so gained, subsequent years' budgets should contain provisions for items of repair or replacements of an ordinary or extraordinary nature. Thus the contributing public of a particular year is asked to contribute only the actual amount needed for repairs and replacements in that year.

"To illustrate the principle, let us use the specific instance of an Association building. The Association has secured from the contributing public of the present generation funds with which to erect and equip a building for the use of the young people of that community. It would be manifestly unfair to again charge this same contributing public in this same generation with an amount that will be set aside as a reserve for depreciation against the day when the building will have to be replaced with a new building and the new building will have to be equipped. In other words, as the present and past generations have provided the existing building and equipment it is neither unwise nor unfair to expect future generations to do as well."

This line of argument is not conclusive. In the absence of a strict definition of "maintaining properties in first class condition," not much can be said about propriety or equity in charging costs. Under the most stringent interpretation of such a phrase, the only possibility of replacement would arise from supersession or inadequacy. But repairs and replacements are never so imminently necessary as to preclude some postponement, and it would seem a difficult question as to when such steps should be taken in the interests of maintaining "first class condition." Thus the annual budget of repairs and replacements would not meet the question of proper charges to operations except upon subjective and somewhat capricious grounds.

But the argument fails to distinguish between investment and operations--between capital and income--and it confuses "expense" of the contributors with expense of the fund. Expense of the fund is the release of services through operations, and this is not the same thing as maintenance of condition of the assets. The original contribution, whatever its source, is an investment of capital (even though it is made without any hope of return in the financial sense); it must not be confused with the operating aspects of depreciation.

Further, the failure to charge depreciation is contradictory to the basic notion of accrual accounting. Depreciation and amortization are part and parcel of accrual accounting; they cannot be avoided by those who profess acceptance of the accrual basis. Accounting on a cash basis, however useful it may be for financial purposes, is a system of record-keeping that has limited function and a restricted usefulness. The argument against the recognition of depreciation as expense in a nonprofit institution confuses the functions of accounting with the exigencies of finance. The source of funds is no criterion as to the method of accounting to be employed for the assets thus brought into the fund; anyway, a "reserve" for depreciation has nothing to do with the flow of funds in any direct sense. The entries for acquisition and operation of fixed assets in a nonprofit institution might be made after the following fashion:

Acquisition:	Capital Fund:		
	Building and equipment............	$2,500,000	
	Capital invested in fixed assets.............		$2,500,000
Depreciation:	Capital Fund:		
	Capital invested in fixed assets......	$ 125,000	
	Allowance for depreciation....................		$ 125,000
	Current Fund:		
	Depreciation of fixed assets (expense).	$ 125,000	
	Capital applied to current operations (equity)....		$ 125,000

Repairs and replacements would be handled through the Capital Fund rather than through the Current Fund, cash being transferred as needed or desired. But whether the cash is transferred or not is a question of financial administration; whether or not new funds are to be solicited is not a matter of gain or loss from operations but rather one of whether new funds are needed.

15. National Committee on Municipal Accounting, op. cit., p. 4.

16. An interesting application of fund theory to a somewhat unusual problem appears in C. Reinold Noyes, "A Consolidated Balance Sheet for a Democracy," Journal of Accountancy, LXXXIII, No. 2 (February, 1947), 100-112.

17. There are criteria other than mere voting control which may be applied to establish the "area" of consolidation. See Maurice Moonitz, The Entity Theory of Consolidated Statements (Bloomington, Ind.: American Accounting Association, 1944), pp. 22-44.

18. "Accounting Questions," Journal of Accountancy, LXXVIII, No. 5 (November, 1944), 424.

19. An interesting illustration of this is the procedure adopted by one affiliation, made up of twenty-five corporations, some of which have at times been less than 100 per cent owned. The accounting for the entire group of companies is not only centralized in one office but is maintained in a single set of records. Although specific accounts are maintained to separate the assets, equities, and operating results of each company, the segregation is not complete; and there is no attempt to maintain separate ledgers for each company. In handling intercompany transactions, the lines of differentiation between legal units is largely ignored. For instance, a transfer of goods from the inventory of one company to that of another is recorded by a charge to one inventory account and a credit to the other one, without reference to intercompany receivable and payable accounts; similarly, an allocation of the general overhead of the parent-company is charged directly into subsidiary accounts, as if they were but departments of the "firm." Though these procedures are covered by necessary legal and financial arrangements, the effect is to ignore intercompany balances so far as day-to-day recording is concerned. Of course, the composite ledger is maintained in equilibrium just as is any other ledger, but at the end of the fiscal period the statements for the legal units may be prepared by merely "balancing" the individual balance sheets with intercompany accounts; the check on this is, of course, that these intercompany balances must offset when taken together. This procedure has been found entirely adequate to produce either the set of statements for individual legal entities or the consolidated reports. Although consolidated reports require some adjustment of the ledger balances, these may be made, without disturbing the ledger balances as recorded, by the use of working paper adjustments comparable to those ordinarily employed when separate statements are consolidated. The legal aspects of intercorporate organization appear to have but a limited effect upon the maintenance of records in this situation.

20. Op. cit., p. 43.

21 Ibid., pp. 90-91.

22. Of course, the "surplus" of the parent-company would vary with the way in which subsidiary income or loss might be handled in the investment and dividend receipts accounts of the parent-company An interesting contrast between three different viewpoints may be drawn in the handling of the investment account in this situation:

One of these views is that subsidiary income or loss should not be recognized on the books of the parent-company at all but that the investment account should be left stated at cost of acquisition. The only source of income to be reflected on the books of the parent-company would be through dividends declared by the subsidiary.

A second view holds that there is good reason for adjusting the investment account to reflect the gains and losses of the subsidiary company. Under this view, profitable operations of the subsidiary would be recognized on the books of the parent-company by the entry:

Investment in subsidiary company..........................	$25,000	
Income from subsidiary operations............................		$25,000

Thus, the income of the subsidiary is reflected on the books of the parent-company specifically, as earned by the subsidiary company. The receipt of dividends, however, is not treated as income but as return of investment, and the entry for a dividend declaration by the subsidiary company would be reflected on the parent-company books by the entry:

Dividends receivable from subsidiary company....	$10,000	
Investment in subsidiary company................................		$10,000

A third position, however, might be maintained; this would follow the second to the extent of recognizing the operations of the subsidiary company but would maintain the restrictive character of undistributed subsidiary surplus. Under this scheme the recognition of subsidiary profits would involve the entry:

Investment in subsidiary company.....................	$25,000	
Majority equity in undistributed subsidiary surplus............		$25,000

and the declaration of dividends by the subsidiary company would be reflected on the parent's books by the following:

Dividends receivable..	$10,000	
Majority equity in undistributed subsidiary surplus.. .	$10,000	
Investment in subsidiary company................................		$10,000
Dividends received from subsidiary (revenue)..................		$10,000

(cf. H. A Finney, Principles of Accounting [New York: Prentice-Hall, Inc., 1936], pp. 282-87).

The first of these viewpoints is an "entity theory" treatment of the problem; since the books of the parent-company are presumed to reflect only those transactions that affect the legal unit, income cannot arise from subsidiary operations except through the formality of declaring dividends in the subsidiary company. Hence the investment account would remain stated at cost to the parent-company, the legal entity for which the books are kept.

The second view is a "proprietary" view; profits of a subsidiary company are obviously determinants of the "net worth" of the majority stockholders. Although the reasons given for preference for the procedure of adjusting the investment account for subsidiary gains and losses are usually based upon the ease with which consolidated reports can be prepared, this argument is really without weight. It really makes little difference whether the investment account is adjusted on the books of the parent, whether such adjustments are made on working papers in preparing the consolidated report, or whether the consolidated statements are prepared by allocating the surplus equities of the various companies without adjusting the parent-company investment account at all. The basis for the "adjusted book value" method is really an espousal of proprietary theory.

The third view is that which evolves from the fund-theory approach to the problem. Earnings of the subsidiary do affect the valuation that may be placed upon the investment in the subsidiary, but such revaluation does not result in income; there still remains the restriction that applies to undistributed surplus of the subsidiary company, and this restriction should be preserved in the books of the parent-company as well as in the final consolidated report.

23. Paton, op. cit., p. 791. Paton discusses a case in which the mutual holdings are, respectively, 70 and 60 per cent. After making the computations so as to show no distinction or division of equity between the two groups of stockholders, he says that both groups are minorities; but he further states: "It would of course be possible to prepare a consolidated statement from the point of view of the M company, ignoring the fact that the assets of R company include an investment in M stock, and then compile a similar statement from the standpoint of the R company, but it is not clear that any proper purpose would be served by such reporting."

24. Moonitz (op. cit., p. 85) recognizes this clearly, as have other writers; but Moonitz says: "Because the term minority interest is so well intrenched, however, a terminological innovation has been avoided in this monograph by employing the more familiar phrase, with 'outside' interest used frequently as the least novel synonym."

25. Control is not merely a matter of majority voting power; "minority interests" frequently place themselves in strategic positions despite their small voting strength. A minority group of less than 5 per cent of the shareholders of White Motor Corporation was able to force Studebaker Corporation into receivership in 1932, despite the previous consummation of an agreement between the corporations by means of which Studebaker acquired control of White. Preemptive and conditional rights, conversion privileges, and other similar provisions in stock contracts may upset "normal" control situations, and suits in equity may have far-reaching effects, even when brought by minority groups.

26 *Op. cit.*, pp. 85-86.

27. *Ibid.*, p. 86.

28. *Ibid.*

29. This point is clearly revealed by the statement in Moonitz (*ibid.* pp. 86-87): "Until records are available for the integrated group wholly independent of the accounts of constituent units, each adjustment made, whether it is admitted or not, is in effect a correction of the accounts of one of affiliated companies." This statement implies that consolidated reports are prepared by adjusting the books of the constituent companies, despite the fact that the position is taken on p. 13 of the same monograph that the consolidated reports are based upon the essential economic unity of an affiliated group. In any event, a consolidated report is supposed to reflect what would appear on a set of records maintained for the consolidated fund, not the individual companies. Whether or not such records are actually maintained is not important to the underlying theory.

30. *Ibid.*, p. 67. Moonitz points out that the amount of good-will may in such cases depend upon whether the parent "costs" investments (made at different prices on various dates) on a "first-in, first-out," or other basis. He cites E. J. B. Lewis, *Consolidated Statements* (New York: Ronald Press, 1942), pp. 61-63, for illustrations of this.

31. This solution follows one pattern presented by W. A. Paton (ed.), *Accountant's Handbook* (3d ed; New York: Ronald Press Co., 1943), pp. 1102-3.

32. This solution follows the procedure outlined in Lewis, *op. cit.*, pp. 171-74.

33. It should be noted that there is another way in which the equations may be set up to allocate the joint equities. Paton (*Advanced Accounting*, pp. 784 ff.) suggests that the equations should be framed to include the capital stock as well as surplus equities but to exclude the intercompany investment. This is, of course, akin to computing the effect of a simultaneous liquidation of both companies at book values. But his discussion does not deal explicitly with the case of acquisitions at prices other than book values on different dates; he implies that this situation would be handled by adjusting the net proprietary interests for the imputed total good-will.

To put the present case on a basis comparable to Paton's discussion, it may first be assumed that the Britic investment in Amerc shares was made at the indicated "book value" of the Amerc equity at that time, $96,000. This "book value" is not computed from the legal balance sheet of Amerc at the date of acquisition but upon the basis of the consolidated statement as it would have appeared just prior to the acquisition of Amerc shares; this is the only way to avoid "good-will" in the final balance sheet of the consolidation.

With the situation thus defined, the net equities of the two classes of stock as reflected on the books of the two companies would be computed:

	Amerc	Britic
Capital stock.	$ 200,000	$200,000
Surplus.	800,000	300,000
Gross equities	1,000,000	500,000
Less: Intercompany investments	160,000	96,000
Net equities.	$ 840,000	$404,000

The equations for allocating these (joint) equities between the two classes of outside stockholders would be:

A = $840,000 + .8B	A = $1,384,761.90	.8A = $1,107,809.52
B = $404,000 + .2A	B = $ 680,952.38	.2B = $ 136,190.48

These results are precisely the same as those obtained by the method presented in the text above, for the sum of the capital stock and surplus equities are identical for each stockholder group. It is curious, however, that the absence of the good-will element should still give the same final equities. It would be expected that the acquisition of Amerc shares at $96,000 instead of $100,000 would dilute the remaining stockholders' equity by a smaller amount and that there would be a correspondingly higher final figure! The fact is that the insertion of the good-will overstated the stock equities by that amount.

If the solution is approached from another position--one that Paton would seem to prefer--the balance-sheet data may be adjusted to reflect the entire good-will valuation of $20,000 (imputed from the purchase of a 20% share of the proprietorship at a price $4,000 in excess of the "book value"); the equations would then be set up as follows:

A = $860,000 + .8B	A = $1,404,761.90	.8A = $1,123 809.52
B = $400,000 + .2A	B = $ 680,952.38	.2B = $ 136,190.48

Again the result is the same as that previously secured, except that the net outside interest in Amerc includes $16,000 "surplus from revaluation of good-will," which is 80 per cent of the total good-will recognized in process of solving the problem.

34. Cf. the treatment of treasury shares in W. A. Paton, Essentials of Accounting (New York: Macmillan Co., 1938), p. 683; and in his Advanced Accounting, pp. 537-51.

35. It is interesting to observe that the same results may be obtained by approaching the problem from the final balance-sheet data rather than following the historical analysis presented in the text:

Step 1.--Allocate the combined equities in the total consolidated surplus as at December 31, 1945, using the equations:

$A = \$800{,}000 + .8B$	$A = \$1{,}238{,}095.24$	$.8A = \$990{,}476.19$
$B = \$300{,}000 + .2A$	$B = \$\ \ 547{,}619.06$	$.2B = \$109{,}523.81$

Step 2.--Calculate the unrestricted equities in the final earned surplus:
Amerc, 80 per cent of \$800,000 = \$640,000; Britic, 20 per cent of \$300,000 = \$60,000
The indicated working paper adjustments needed to reclassify the surplus equities are:

Earned surplus, Amerc	\$800,000.00	
Earned surplus, Britic	300,000.00	
Amerc equity in unrestricted earned surplus		\$640,000.00
Britic equity in unrestricted earned surplus		60,000.00
Amerc equity in undistributed consolidated surplus		350,476.19
Britic equity in undistributed consolidated surplus		49,523.81

Step 3.--The elimination of intercompany investment effects: The investment of Amerc in Britic is simply canceled against the reciprocal capital stock element:

Capital stock, Britic	\$160,000 00	
Investment in Britic		\$160,000 00

The other investment account represents a purchased equity in surplus as well as in the capital stock. The surplus equities as at the date of acquisition may be allocated by the equations:

$A = \$200{,}000 + .8B$	$A = \$333{,}333.33$	$.8A = \$266{,}666.67$
$B = \$100{,}000 + .2A$	$B = \$166{,}666.67$	$.2B = \$\ 33{,}333.33$

From these figures must be deducted the amount of earned surplus as it existed before the acquisition:

Amerc: 80 per cent of (\$200,000 + 80 per cent of \$100,000) = \$224,000.00
Britic: 20 per cent of \$100,000 = \$ 20,000.00

The indicated elimination entry is:

Capital stock, Amerc	\$ 40,000.00	
Amerc equity in undistributed consolidated surplus	42,666.67	
Britic equity in undistributed consolidated surplus	13,333.33	
Good-will--suspense	4,000.00	
Investment in Amerc		\$100,000 00

It will be noted that it is the change in surplus equities brought about by the acquisition of Amerc shares that is eliminated. The earned surplus not eliminated is the amount of accumulated earnings up to the date of Amerc share acquisition; this is as it should be, for such earnings as they apply to the present shareholders are perfectly legitimate surplus equities even though they remain undistributed.

Step 4.--The good-will suspense item is written off, as explained in the text:

Amerc equity in unrestricted earned surplus	\$ 3,809.52	
Britic equity in unrestricted earned surplus	190.48	
Good-will, suspense		\$ 4,000.00

The effects of these "adjustments" may be tabulated as follows:

Entry	Amerc Equities		Britic Equities	
	Unrestricted Earned Surplus	Undistributed Equity in Consolidated Surplus	Unrestricted Earned Surplus	Undistributed Equity in Consolidated Surplus
Step 2--To set up gross equities as at December 31, 1945...	$640,000.00	$350,476.19	$60,000.00	$49,523.81
Step 3--To subtract the effect of the acquisition transaction in Amerc shares...		42,666.67*		13,333.33*
Step 4--To subtract the write-off of "good-will--suspense"..	3,809.52*		190.48*	
Net equities, as per consolidated balance sheet, 12-31-45........	$636,190.48	$307,809.52	$59,809.52	$36,190.48

*Deduction.

36. Paton, Advanced Accounting, p. 752; see also Moonitz, op. cit., pp. 10-21, 73-78. Moonitz does not take a clear position as between the alternatives proposed in Solutions I and II; he seems, however, to suggest a preference for the "treasury stock" approach adopted in Solution I.

CHAPTER V

1. William H. Whitney, "What is a Balance Sheet?" Journal of Accountancy, LXX, No. 4 (October, 1940), 293-308.

2. Accounting Research Bulletin No. 9 (New York: Committee on Accounting Procedure, American Institute of Accountants, 1941), pp. 68-69.

3. Ibid., p. 70.

4. Ibid., pp. 70-71.

5. Ibid., p. 76.

6. F. W. Woodbridge, "Time as a Factor in Determining Debt-paying Ability," Accounting Review, XIV, No. 3 (September, 1939), 236-50.

7. James L. Dohr, "What Is an Asset?" Journal of Accountancy, LXXIII, No. 3 (March, 1942), 213-18.

8. George O. May, Financial Accounting (New York: Macmillan Co., 1943), p. 27: "In England, the larger enterprises, such as canals, railways, and other companies. . . . follow the double account system of accounting." (My italics)

9. Lawrence R. Dicksee, Advanced Accounting, (7th ed; London: Gee & Co , 1932), p. 149. He points out in a footnote that "under the Companies Act, 1929 (sec. 124-1) companies are now required to frame their balance sheets so as to distinguish between fixed assets and floating assets, but they are not yet obliged to adopt the Double Account form, and in practice rarely do so." Later in the text, however (p. 150), he points out that the double-account system of accounting is mandatory for railways, gas and water companies, and local authorities--in fact, for any companies that are incorporated by special act of Parliament.

10. F. N. Keen, The Law Relating to Public Service Undertakings (London: P. S. King & Son, Ltd., 1925), pp. 73-74.

11. Op. cit., p. 153.

12. Alfred Nixon and J. H. Stagg, Accounting and Banking (London: Longmans, Green & Co., 1907), p. 303. It is worth noting the implication of carrying forward the balance of what we would call a "Repairs and Renewals Reserve" as a "liability." If this is regarded as a liability, it suggests that the separate fund entity of current and capital operations is more than a mere imaginary device. Further, it would tend to support our position that equities (at least in this instance) represent restrictions upon assets, not legal obligations.

13. Ibid., p. 294.

14. Cf. W. A. Paton's statement (Essentials of Accounting [New York: Macmillan Co., 1938], p. 544): "Organization costs should be retained as a permanent asset as long as the business maintains a substantially unimpaired status as a going concern, as reflected in earning power and tangible resources, and should be amortized with a sustained contraction of income and tangible assets resulting from either a lack of operating success or deliberate liquidation. Thus in the case of a continuing vigorous enterprise the costs of organizing the business are not subject to amortization." The same statement appears in his Advanced Accounting. (New York: Macmillan Co., 1941), p. 414.

15. Above, Chap. V. n. 1.

16. Nixon and Stagg, op. cit., p. 302.

17. Donald Kehl, Corporate Dividends (New York: Ronald Press Co., 1941), pp. 126-28.

18. Nixon and Stagg, op. cit , p. 303.

19. Ibid.

20. Prosper Reiter, Profits, Dividends and the Law (New York: Ronald Press Co., 1926), pp. 24-25, 50-51. Henry Rand Hatfield (Modern Accounting [New York: D. Appleton & Co., 1909], p. 202) writes: "Doubtless, because of being accustomed in double accounts to treat capital as a thing by itself, the English courts have been more ready to take advanced ground on the general problem."

21. Ibid., pp. 201-2. There are several other references in Hatfield's work to the double-account notion; one of the illustrative forms of balance sheets presented is that of the Atchison, Topeka & Santa Fe Railway Company System, dated June 30, 1902. This is in double-account form, except that the transposition of assets and equities mentioned previously in the text is amended to follow the American practice. Hatfield's reference to probate accounting with respect to the separation of capital and revenue items is now somewhat out of date, at least so far as depreciation charges are concerned. See Joseph Hartwig, "Should the Accountant Depreciate Investment Buildings Held by Trustees under Testamentary Trusts?" Journal of Business,XVIII, No. 1 (January, 1945), 41-55. The conclusion reached in Hartwig's study is that "depreciation is required in some cases; it is permitted in others, and it should be the rule and not the exception."

22. Paul Joseph Esquerré, Applied Theory of Accounts (New York: Ronald Press Co., 1914), pp. 412-13.

23. Roy B. Kester, Accounting Theory and Practice (2d ed.; New York: Ronald Press Co., 1925), pp. 77-79.

24. English accountants, of course, still present discussions of the double-account statement and the accompanying system of procedures in many of their textbooks, because the system of accounting is still legally prescribed for parliamentary companies. On occasion, some discussion of this subject creeps into periodical literature. Cf., e.g., Francis W. Pixley (ed.), The Accountant's Dictionary (3d ed.; London: New Era Publishing Company, Ltd., 1931[?]), I, 302-5, 436-43, 412-13; George Lisle, Accounting Theory and Practice (Edinburgh and London: William Green & Sons, 1909), pp. 79-82; R. N. Carter (ed.), Advanced Accounts (New York: E. P. Dutton & Co.), pp. 454-55, 908-12; Dicksee, op. cit., pp. 149-54; T. F. Brennan, "The Double Account System," Accountant, LX, No. 2323 (June 14, 1919), 509-15.

25. William Morse Cole, "Our Outdated Accounting," Harvard Business Review,XI, No. 4 (July, 1933), 482-89.

26. William A. Paton, Recent and Prospective Developments in Accounting Theory ("Harvard University Business Research Studies," No. 25 [Boston, April, 1940]), p. 7.

27. New York: American Institute of Accountants, 1920.

28. W. A. Paton (ed.), *The Accountant's Handbook* (New York: Ronald Press Co., 1932), pp. 19-20.

29. *Ibid.*, (3d ed.; New York: Ronald Press Co., 1943), p. 9.

30. *Ibid.*, p. 7.

31. *Op. cit.*, p. 243.

32. Caterpillar Tractor Company, Annual Report, 1944, p. 23.

33. August L. Knollmuller, "The Application of Funds Statement," *Journal of Accountancy*, LV, No. 2 (February, 1933), 101-7; Harry L. Kunze, "A New Form of Funds Statement," *Accounting Review*, XV, No. 2 (June, 1940), 222-25; *Accountant's Handbook* (3d ed.), p. 102.

34. John B. Canning, *The Economics of Accounting* (New York: Ronald Press Co., 1929) pp. 207-8. (My italics.)

35. Emphasis upon the desirability and the "objectivity" of cash transcends accounting literature (see, e.g., W. A. Paton and A. C. Littleton, *An Introduction to Corporate Accounting Standards* [Chicago: American Accounting Association, 1940], pp. 24, 27, 29, 37, 41, 57-59, *et passim*)

36. John Maynard Keynes, *A Treatise on Money* (New York: Harcourt, Brace & Co., 1930), p. 3.

37. *Ibid.*, pp. 53 ff.

38. *Ibid.*, pp. 53-120. J. R. Hicks, *Value and Capital* (Oxford: Clarendon Press, 1939), pp. 11-52.

39. H. W. Sweeney, *Stabilized Accounting* (New York: Harper & Bros., 1936); cf. Robert L. Dixon, Jr., "The Income Statement" (unpublished doctoral dissertation, Yale University, 1941). Professor Dixon presents the novel idea of bringing together changes in the general price level and the fluctuations in a special "entity index" made up from the prices of goods and services purchased by the business firm.

40. Objectivity is sometimes taken to mean "impersonalness," "externality," "absence of bias," or "reliance upon facts." To accept these definitions or to take the position that accountants should be concerned only with "impartial" observation and reporting of facts is really to beg the question of what is meant by objectivity.

All interpretations of data are made from experience, and all facts are but generalizations from experience. "All knowledge is personal in the sense that what we perceive or are able to perceive is largely a matter of the "apperceptive mass," and this involves both expectations and interests" (Frank H. Knight, "What Is Truth in Economics?" *Journal of Political Economy*, XLVIII, No. 1, [February, 1940], 11). The important element in an "objective" representation is that the experience to which given data are referred for interpretation must be a "social" experience; else the representation cannot carry meaning to the recipient. Objectivity is the *agreement* of intelligent persons as to the significance of independently observed data; it implies not only separate experience or observation on the part of different individuals but also a communal reporting of those observations, attempts to differentiate those separate impressions, and, when the group can make no differentiation between the individual reports, a final agreement as to the unanimity of the separate experiences. Objectivity is a social, not an individual, phenomenon; its significance is relative, depending upon the amount of agreement that arises from the processes which have been described. There is nothing objective in any datum or observation per se; "the essence of the idea of objectivity is conscious social consensus" (*ibid.*, p. 7).

To emphasize some one basis of valuation is not necessarily objective, for every valuation is related to the situation in which it is made and the purpose which it is to serve. True objectivity would seem better served by recognizing different bases of valuation as alternatives that may have special significance to some and less significance to other readers, since the situations and problems involved are different. Certainly, there should be no restriction upon the judgment of the accountant, to prevent his using valuation tools to promote those purposes to which the financial presentations will be devoted.

41. Cf. Chester Martin, "Do We Need a Balance Sheet?" *Journal of Accountancy*, LXXV, No. 4 (April, 1943), 343-47.

CHAPTER VI

1. W. A. Paton, Advanced Accounting (New York: Macmillan Co., 1941), p. 19. In substantially the same terms, this statement also appears in his Essentials of Accounting (New York: Macmillan Co., 1938), p. 752.

2. "Nature and Purpose of the Income Statement," Journal of Accountancy, LXXX, No. 3 (September, 1945), 205.

3. Cf. Accounting for Income Taxes: Accounting Research Bulletin No. 23 (New York: American Institute of Accountants, December, 1944), pp. 183-94; and Securities and Exchange Commission, In the Matter of Charges in Lieu of Taxes ("Accounting Series Release," No. 53 [Washington, D.C.: The Commission, November 16, 1945]).

4. Advanced Accounting, pp. 598-600.

5. W. A. Paton and A. C. Littleton, An Introduction to Corporate Accounting Standards (Chicago: American Accounting Association, 1940), p. 67.

6. Robert L. Dixon, Jr., "Fixed and Variable Costs," Accounting Review, XV, No. 2 (June, 1940), 219. (My italics.)

7. Charles F. Schlatter, "Fixed Expense," Accounting Review, XX, No. 2 (April, 1945), 161. The last part of the last paragraph arises from the viewpoints expressed by Clem N. Kohl, "What Is Wrong with Most Profit and Loss Statements?" Bulletin of the National Association of Cost Accountants, Vol. XVIII, No. 1, Part I (July 1, 1937), and to "G. Charter Harrison's contention that Profit and Loss Statements are in error if they show an increase in profit because of an increase in production without a corresponding increase in sales" (p. 159).

8. Schlatter, op. cit., p 161.

9. Arundel Cotter, Fool's Profits (New York: Barron's Publishing Co., 1940).

10. George G. Rinder, "Investment Standards of Profit and Loss" (unpublished Master's report, University of Chicago, School of Business, 1942), pp. 19-34.

11. Proctor and Gamble Company, Annual Report, June 30, 1938, p. 4.

12. John B. Canning, The Economics of Accounting (New York: Ronald Press Co., 1929), p. 98.

13. Op. cit., p. 205.

14. Op. cit., p. 141.

15. American Institute of Accountants, Contemporary Accounting (New York: The Institute, 1945), chap 3, pp. 8-9.

16. Advanced Accounting, pp. 438-39.

17. The managerial emphasis in the field of cost accounting (mentioned in the last quotation) is described only partially therein. Cost accountants and comptrollers have shown extreme interest in devices and methods which have little or no expression in the income statement. Examples are the detailed analysis of costs and revenues by lines of product, territories, administrative and functional units of organization; special procedural and strategic analyses directed at specific issues of managerial objectives and policy; budgetary control and the aspects of forecasting and internal reporting allied thereto; fixed and variable, controllable, differential, and other special classifications and interpretations of operating data. This meaning of "managerial" accounting has not been advanced explicitly in many writings on accounting, yet it seems perfectly obvious to those who view the accounting system from within enterprise areas. The managerial uses of accounting arise largely from the analectic character of accounting information, which lends itself readily to the preparation of informative reports on specific subjects of many different kinds. The major purposes of management would probably be more hindered than helped by limiting accounting information for these purposes to the "general ledger" aspects of transactions or by emphasizing the income statement data in such connections. Peculiarly, it is the interpretive or alternative aspect of transactions taken in detail that has significance for the processes of management.

18. Paton, Advanced Accounting, p. 678. It should be made clear, however, that not even the statement of funds gives a report of all the transactions which affect the balance sheet. Paton goes on to say that "it endeavors to trace the entire flow of financing and operation, in the broadest sense, insofar as these processes contact the working capital section of the business structure."

19. Journal of Accountancy, LXIII, No. 5 (May, 1937), 363.

20. Maurice Moonitz, "Inventories and the Statement of Funds," Accounting Review, XVIII, No. 3 (July, 1943), 262

21. Accountant's Handbook (3d ed.; New York: Ronald Press Co., 1943), p. 98.

22. Caterpillar Tractor Company, Annual Report, 1944, pp. 24-25.

23. The very name of this statement is a source of some confusion. Starting from the "where-got, where-gone" title employed by Cole, this statement has been called "Statement of Application of Funds," "Statement of Funds--Sources and Applications," "Summary of Changes in Net Current Assets," and "Statement Accounting for Variations in Working Capital."

24. Paton, Essentials of Accounting, p. 798, carries the suggestion that the fund statement "is not a statement of receipts and disbursements, but it focusses attention upon the current funds phase of the outstanding activities."

25. Hiram T. Scovill, "Application of Funds Made Practical," Accounting Review, XIX, No. 1 (January, 1944), 21. (My italics.)

26. Perry Mason, Fundamentals of Accounting (Chicago: Foundation Press, 1942), p. 416. It is interesting to contrast this quotation with the position taken by William H. Whitney, "What Is a Balance Sheet?" Journal of Accountancy, LXX, No. 4 (October, 1940), esp. pp. 302-3.

27. J. B. Taylor and Herman C. Miller, Intermediate Accounting (New York: McGraw-Hill Book Co., 1938), p. 72. The last sentence appears in a footnote.

28. George O. May, "Improvement in Financial Accounts," op. cit , p. 364.

29. It would seem a reasonably acceptable hypothesis that the income statement itself had its origin in the changes in "net worth" emphasized under proprietary theory. See A. C Littleton, Accounting Evolution to 1900 (New York: American Institute Publishing Company, 1933), pp. 132-35.

30. Moonitz, (op. cit., p. 263) writes: "Paton, and Myer as well, develop a procedure consistent with the identity of working capital....and funds. The result is a statement that accounts for variation in working capital which may be useful in its own right, but not as a statement of the flow of funds." Scovill (op. cit., p. 23) states: "Some writers in dealing with application of funds statements are inconsistent in that they add non-cash debits to the net profit result but do not deduct any non-cash credits." This argues for the cash notion of the statement, but the conversion of the income statement to one of cash receipts and disbursements would be a very tedious process; and the result ought, if such be the case, to be called by its appropriate title of "Statement of Cash Receipts and Disbursements," not "Application of Funds Statement."

31. Presumably, some case could be claimed for an alternative treatment which would recognize the trade-in and the acquisition of the new machine as two separate transactions; such an approach would result in a "provision of funds" in the amount of $1,000 representing the trade-in value of the old machine, and an "application of funds" amounting to $5,000, the agreed price of the new machine. The entries would be!

Current Fund:		
Trade-in suspense	$1,000	
Current residual equity		$1,000

Capital Fund:		
Net working capital	$1,000	
Allowance for depreciation of machinery	$2,000	
Machinery		$3,000

to record the trade-in of the old machine; then, to record the acquisition of the new item, the entries would be set:

Current Fund:		
Transfer to capital fund for new machinery	$5,000	
Trade-in suspense		$1,000
Instalment notes payable		$4,000

Capital Fund:		
Machinery	$5,000	
Net working capital		$5,000

However, it is awkward to show the trade-in transaction as an increase in net working capital, even though this state is but a transient one; the treatment shown in the text is to be preferred.

32. It should be observed that the pattern of entries presented in the text above makes the effects of depreciation charges upon the current position easier to understand. In the first instance, depreciation charges do affect the amount of working assets, because the depreciation charge is added to inventory valuations. But, to the extent that the goods in process are completed and sold in the same period in which the depreciation is booked, the final effect upon working assets is really zero; the inventory costs (including depreciation) are transferred to expense. When some of the inventory remains unsold, some of the valuation effect remains in the balance sheet, which tends to increase the amount of working assets. This effect, however, is partially or completely offset by carry-overs of depreciation at the beginning of the fiscal period. The only way in which depreciation charges really change the current asset picture is this inventory valuation effect.

That part of the depreciation charge which is transferred to expense, on the other hand, represents a restriction or reservation against the current assets, for it is nothing more than a recovery of the capital cost transferred to current operations and thence to the market transaction which produce the revenue; it operates to "reserve" some of the current assets in the sense of maintaining the obligation to the capital fund. There is thus a real justification for regarding the current fund credit in the depreciation entry as an equity element in the sense of a liability to the capital fund (see above, p. 300, for the English recommendation to this effect). If this approach were followed, the depreciation charge could be allowed to remain unadjusted as a deduction from revenue in the income statement, so far as the statement of funds is concerned, because the initial entry for depreciation would not result in an increase in the residual equity but would be shown as a specific equity, representing the transfers of fixed capital cost to current operations.

The statement is sometimes carelessly made that depreciation charges assist or affect the financing of current operations. Of course it is true that even during periods in which heavy losses are sustained, net working capital may increase despite the absence of new investment (see Arthur H. Winakor, Maintenance of Working Capital of Industrial Corporations by Conversion of Fixed Assets ["University of Illinois Research Bulletin," No. 49 (Urbana: University of Illinois, 1934)]). But the amounts that actually find their way into net working capital balances really arise from revenue--not from depreciation charges--except for the small inventory effect that has been mentioned. The depreciation charge really operates to impound in the current fund (for or without regard to expended reinvestment in capital assets) that portion of assets arising from revenue which represents recovery of capital cost. Thus depreciation is not a source of funds, nor does the conversion of fixed assets operate to increase working funds; rather, the effect is to maintain the net working capital by impounding the capital cost recoveries in the current fund.

33. See the solutions presented to Problem 2, Part II, of the American Institute Examination in "Accounting Theory and Practice" of May, 1943, in Journal of Accountancy, LXXVI, No. 3 (September, 1943), 268 ff.; Accounting Review, XVIII, No. 4 (October, 1943), 374 ff.

34. Paton, Advanced Accounting, p. 682. A complete illustration of this form is presented as a concrete example in his Essentials of Accounting, pp. 801-4.

35. Cf. Paton and Littleton, op. cit., pp. 84-89.

36. It is interesting to speculate what would be the result if this form were applied to a situation involving a net decrease in the net working capital during the fiscal period. To be sure, the form does provide for this; a caption appears within the form which would be used, if there were need for it; but in such case, the final amount at the end of the statement would be zero. To insert "nil" in this final space would seem to be contradictory; further, it might suggest that the last-mentioned expenditures were made in view of the amount made available by the decrease in net working capital, when the real state of affairs is quite the reverse. However, no form can be devised to cover all situations with complete adequacy; the advantages of standardization are soon dissipated if the principle of uniformity is carried to extremes.

37. The illustration presented here is taken from Paton, Essentials of Accounting, pp. 801 ff.

38. In chap. i the position was taken that a theory of accounting should not of itself involve commitment to any particular set of premises as to methods of valuation. It was stated there that this discussion would not be concerned with valuation, except as to how valuation procedures might have an effect upon the uses or the applications of fund theory. Consequently, we have discussed depreciation and amortization in terms of cost valuations and annual charges to amortize cost. The omission of alternative approaches to the statement of depreciation or other charges transferred from capital to current account arises from the desire to maintain simplicity in the illustration and to avoid a confusion of issues between valuation methods and the theoretical structure with which this discussion is concerned.

However, there is no conclusive reason for confining the computation of depreciation or other capital charges to a strict cost basis. Depreciation or other "amortization" charges might be viewed as "usage charges" for those services withdrawn from capital assets and applied to operations for the period; this usage charge could easily be made to reflect current price levels. For instance, plant assets which cost $100,000 and which are subject to a depreciation rate of 5 per cent per annum would entail depreciation charges of $5,000 per year. Supposing that an appraisal indicates that the present reproduction cost, new of these plant assets is $150,000, there could also be shown with the depreciation charge of $5,000 an additional $2,500 to supplement the cost amortization and to provide for the fact that current dollars of depreciation are not the same kind of dollars as are transferred from the plant asset cost via the allowance for depreciation. The $2,500 charge, however, would be reported specifically and would be credited to an equity account in the capital fund, perhaps to be called a "Reserve for Price-Level Fluctuations." This account would then represent the difference between the total cost amortizations and the dollar values (current when the services were transferred to operations) of fixed asset services transferred to current fund operations. In other words, the reserve account would indicate the amount by which operations have "recaptured" price-level effects as these apply to fixed asset amortizations.

Similarly, there is no reason why the amount of the price-level adjustment could not be revised as often as deemed expedient, so as to reflect current shifts in the level of fixed asset replacement costs. This might even be done annually, if there is reason to believe that the amounts thus measured are significant and if there is a basis for making the indicated calculations with some assurance of validity in the result. But the depreciation or amortization would still be shown as including two elements: (*a*) the amortization of cost and (*b*) the correction for price-level fluctuation. The reader of the statement might then include in his calculation of income either the cost amortization alone or the combined charge including the price-level correction, as might best fit the situation and the problem under consideration.

It should be noted that this procedure does not involve "recording" the appraisal, nor does it involve an amortization of appraisal surplus; it results in showing not merely the depreciation on appraised values, but *both* the amortization of cost and the correction for price-level adjustment. See W. A. Paton, *Advanced Accounting*, pp. 325-38, 731-48, for discussion of some of the issues involved in the problem of shifting price levels as these affect fixed asset accounting.

CHAPTER VII

1. See above, Chap. VI.

2. There is no provision in this illustration for a valuation of inventory based on a "lower of cost or market" approach based upon individual *items* in the inventory. This procedure, which yields a total valuation smaller than either aggregate cost or aggregate market, is really an ultraconservative approach to the problem, which in this writer's opinion is undesirable; not only is the figure thus obtained an anomalous one with respect to theories of income but such a valuation is seldom if ever capable of interpretation unless access is had to that great mass of detail which underlies the computation. However, if the reason for doing so were sufficiently important, the effect of this or even other alternative valuations might be shown by the use of additional adjunct or contra accounts.

3. "Surplus" is an unsatisfactory term even in conventional reports. See American Institute of Accountants, *Accounting Research Bulletin No. 12* (New York: The Institute, 1941), pp. 107-9.

4. American Institute of Accountants, *Research Bulletin No. 5* (New York: The Institute, 1940), pp. 41-42.

5. Cf. W. A. Paton, *Advanced Accounting* (New York: Macmillan Co., 1941), p. 639: "Bonds which have been purchased from corporate funds deposited for the purpose represent liabilities effectively discharged and should be reported accordingly. The fact that payment has been made indirectly through a corporate representative and that the bonds are included in the nominal amount of the fund does not justify any other interpretation. If desired, a special contra-account similar to treasury bonds may be employed but again it is good practice to adjust the main liability account directly.

"Is the essential condition changed if interest is regularly 'paid' on bonds held in the sinking fund? A negative answer is required. Where the periodic fund deposit has been calculated on the assumption that the entire accumulation will be invested in earning assets throughout the life of the fund, the use of the fund to acquire outstanding bonds will make necessary other payments by the corporation, to offset the reduction in earning power resulting from such expenditures, if the original program of accumulation is to be maintained; and including the 'interest' on company bonds held by the trustee in periodic deposits of interest money may be a convenient way of contributing the required additional amounts for retirement purposes. The bonds held are nevertheless not truly outstanding and payment of interest is purely a formality of fund accumulation. The charge to bond interest on the corporation's books should be restricted to interest on securities actually outstanding and the balance of the interest money should be charged directly to the sinking fund."

6. It will be noted also, by comparison with the conventional statements, that the 19X2 sinking-fund operations include none of the "discount on purchase of bonds" shown in the entity approach as an increase in surplus (indeed, as a "gain") from retirement of bonds. Rather, the fund approach follows usual investment accounting procedures to report the amortization of premium or the accumulation of discount on securities which are, so far as the fund view goes, no different from other investments.

Paton does grant one exception in which the treatment adopted here perhaps would be acceptable. He says (ibid): "A different treatment might be supported were the trustee granted authority to sell as well as to buy company bonds in connection with fund operations. In such a situation the bonds acquired by the trustee would--somewhat like other securities in which fund deposits were invested--be outside the control of the corporation and might be viewed as contingently if not actually outstanding." This would seem to be taking a position that the trustee is the agent of the corporation in operating the sinking fund; yet Paton is careful to note that, in at least one situation, "it has been held that failure of the trustee to make payment (to the bondholders) does not compel the issuing corporation to make good the default and that the loss falls upon the bondholders" (p. 640). In any event, the treatment of reacquisitions as retirements of the main liability would appear somewhat open to question from the viewpoint of the bondholders who read financial statements. To show as "sinking fund" only those amounts not invested in bonds of the issue gives an incomplete picture of the relative security afforded the bondholders by the operations of the sinking fund.

7. John B. Canning, The Economics of Accountancy (New York: Ronald Press Co., 1929), p. 140.